To_____

From_____
Date_____

Note:_____

_____

_____

_____

_____

Self Help?
No Thanks,
I Can Do It Myself

Self Help?
No Thanks,
I Can Do It Myself

Surviving Life's Journey

By

Dorothy Louise Gagnon

iUniverse, Inc.
New York   Bloomington

Self Help? No Thanks, I Can Do It Myself
Surviving Life's Journey

iUniverse books may be ordered through booksellers or by contacting:

iUniverse
1663 Liberty Drive
Bloomington, IN 47403
www.iuniverse.com
1-800-Authors (1-800-288-4677)

Because of the dynamic nature of the Internet, any Web addresses or links contained in this book may have changed since publication and may no longer be valid. The views expressed in this work are solely those of the author and do not necessarily reflect the views of the publisher, and the publisher hereby disclaims any responsibility for them.

ISBN: 978-1-4401-2016-9 (pbk)
ISBN: 978-1-4401-2017-6 (cloth)
ISBN: 978-1-4401-2018-3 (ebk)

Library of Congress Control Number: 2009921075

Printed in the United States of America

iUniverse rev. date: 3/16/2009

The experiences expressed in this book reflect only the opinions and perceptions of the author.

Dedication

In memory of my son, Brad

1971-1990

and
My dad, Francis

1905–1968

Many times throughout this life of stormy weather
I have felt as inconsequential as a feather
With no control over anything in my world
Just blowing and drifting

Dorothy Louise

Acknowledgments

My special thanks to my husband, Bruce, who has encouraged me and who has been there every step of the way over the past thirty-nine years, and to my daughter, Andrea, who has allowed me to share parts of her own painful and personal story.

I want to express my appreciation to my four wonderful sisters, Lois, Helen, Betty, and Mona, who have been such a major part of my life and who I am eternally grateful to for their part in the person that I have become. Their support has been unwavering, and I can only hope that they are proud of their handiwork.

And last but not least, I would like to thank all of my family and friends who have been so instrumental in teaching me a lot of those life lessons, even when they weren't aware of it!

Contents

I Think the Angels Wrote This for Me

I first heard this poem at a memorial service at Thornton Cemetery in 2005. Something about it resonated deep inside of me, and is so fitting for my own reasons in writing this book.

A Prayer for Spring

Like springtime, let me unfold
And grow, fresh and new,
From this cocoon of grief
That has been spun around me

Help me face the harsh reality of
Sunshine and renewed life
As my bones still creak from
The winter of my grief

Life has dared to go on around me
And as I recover from
The insult of life's continuance
I re-adjust my focus to
Include recovery and growth
As a possibility in my future

Give me strength to break out of
The cocoon of my grief
But may I never forget it as
The place where I grew my wings
Becoming a new person
Because of my loss

Heill, Janis, 1988. *Bittersweet … Hellogoodbye*
Lamb, Sr.Marie. Charis Communications, Illinois. p 60.

Monday, April 11, 2005—11:05 PM

It's one of those blustery, cold, and rainy nights in late spring when all you want to do is curl up with a good book in a big, comfy chair in front of the fireplace. That would be my normal routine on one of these nights when I finally get my housework done and can sit for a bit, but lately that damn little voice in the back of my mind refuses to go away. Because it won't leave me alone, I've finally decided to give in to it. This voice is telling me that it is time to put my life story in some sort of order. For quite a while now, the voice has been getting louder, and it constantly nags me to share my story. When I question the validity or the benefits of sharing my life, this same voice points out that it may help others to realize that, even though life sometimes really sucks, if we look at our choices, learn to accept our fate, and rely on our unique coping skills, then we can become our authentic selves and find some peace.

I certainly do not expect my story to be the great Canadian novel, but, whatever or whoever this voice is, it is telling me that I cannot rest until I have told my story. I am fully aware that my major reason for ignoring this voice has been the fear of revisiting many painful and emotionally challenging times. I also question whether I want to expose my innermost thoughts to all and sundry, essentially airing my dirty laundry in public; however, like many of the pathways that we find ourselves on in this life, the signposts are pointing forward, and I've finally decided to pay attention.

Walk with me for a while. I'm not sure where we'll end up, but, by the time we get there, you might just find something that will help you on your own journey.

Chapter 1
In the Beginning

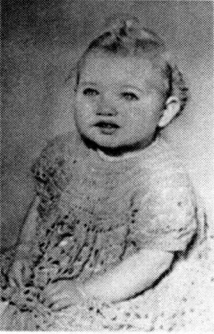

Have you ever asked yourself, "What is the purpose of my life?" I have, and that little voice inside my head that I've decided to call Louie always gives the same answer: "I'll be damned if I know." It sometimes makes me wonder if Louie is my gut instinct or just a lazy bum who has a cozy little home inside my head and doesn't like to do too much thinking. Whatever or whoever he is doesn't matter anymore, because we've become accustomed to each other.

There is one thing that Louie and I do agree on, and that is that absolutely everyone has a story to tell, and we've decided to tell ours. Don't get me wrong, I'm really not some crackpot, and, for the most part during my story, I will refer to myself in the first person. But I have to admit that, as he's developed, Louie has provided me with a strange comedic relief. Who knows, maybe it's because I am a Gemini and a twin side of me had to show up somewhere along the line. Most people who know me think I'm the most level-headed, down-to-earth, and stable person that they have ever known, and generally they are right. Most of them have also experienced my innate—and almost always available—goofy side.

Yet there is one aspect of myself that I don't need Louie for, and that is my physical, mental, spiritual, and emotional freedom. I need my independence as much as I need air to breathe, and that independence includes being totally responsible for my feelings and perceptions about life, accepting that those same thoughts and feelings are just as important and just as valid as anyone else's . For most of my life it seemed that I was not supposed to have my own opinions or if I did, they weren't really important enough for others to take seriously. I thought that reading self help books could fix me so I bought and read almost everything that I could get my hands on that would make me a better person It took a lot of reading and a long time for me to realize that I was already okay. Essentially I had to fix myself and in order for that to happen, I had to believe in myself. I came to understand that I really did have value and it didn't come from a book. The books that I read provided me with a lot of knowledge but it was much like buying a treadmill, setting it in a room, and expecting to get fit. All the books and equipment in the world are only useful if you're actually using them as intended. I'm still in the process of getting 'it' whatever 'it' is but have come to the unequivocal conclusion that I can do it myself. Some people may not agree with me, but that's okay, because I take full responsibility for such feelings, and they are mine and mine alone.

I believe that we live many lives and that we choose the family and life that we are born into in order to learn valuable lessons during each lifetime. I also believe that once we have chosen our lives, we then drink deeply from the waters of forgetfulness before making our way into a womb to begin the wondrous, frightening, and challenging journey on this Earth. Many times during this life, I have asked myself, "If this is true, why on Earth would I have picked such an emotionally difficult life?" At fifty-five years old, I feel twice that age mentally and have many times wished this lifetime was over. But here I am, more than a half of a century later and with no end in sight.

My personal thinking around life continues with the idea that upon entering the womb, our spirit brings with it some karma from our past, and that same spirit continues to be susceptible to what is happening in our psyche every step on the way to birth. I am positive that the fact that I was an unwanted pregnancy, and consequently an unwanted child, has plagued me all my life and continues to be a factor in my reluctance to integrate into a group. This dysfunctional thinking has continuously led me to believe that I have nothing of value to offer in a conversation.

Even now, when I do become part of a group, there swirling around inside my head are negative thoughts, such as "you're not interesting enough," or "you're not smart enough." Consequently, I mask these feelings by either being an authority on whatever the subject matter is or by making smart-ass remarks that are sometimes inappropriate and later come back to haunt me. Because these are traits that I dislike in other people, I'm constantly second-guessing my actions. Perhaps it's true that when you see others acting in a certain way and you become critical of their actions, it's because you are fighting those same demons.

Although there is no concrete evidence, other than DNA testing on a corpse, according to stories told by a few of my aunts and uncles and by my biological mother, I am a product of one of my grandfather's frequent carnal urges. Although my grandmother denied it until the end, there was at least doubt, because at one point, when I was once again trying to pry some information from her, she said, "If it did happen, it was probably Pauline's [my mother's] fault, because she was always throwing herself at men, and, after all, your grandfather was just a man, and men can't help themselves!" Now isn't that the most insane statement you have ever heard?

The stories that I was told much later in life, when I was seeking validation about my mother's version of what happened, came at my nephew's first Communion party. As I asked questions, bits of information began coming forth, and I learned that my grandfather was not only incestuous with my mother, but plied my grandmother with liquor and then lined the kids up inside the bedroom to watch and learn "what you were supposed to do." I got the notion that it was not just the females of the family who were abused, but it was a question that has not been asked up to this point.

Can you imagine the hullabaloo that must have occurred when my mother announced that she was pregnant with me? I do know that she was thrown out of the family home and somehow ended up marrying a man named Raymond in Regina, Saskatchewan, mere days before I was born. From the report that I received from the Children's Aid Society in 1982, there is no known information about my father.

The story as I have been told it is that my mother became pregnant again when I was four months old, this time by her husband, Raymond. He was in the Canadian Forces, and, when Pauline was seven months pregnant, he left her and returned to Nova Scotia. My mother likes to tell the story of how she hitchhiked from Regina, Saskatchewan, to Sydney Mines, Nova Scotia, to make him live up to his responsibilities. It was around this time that my sister Mona was born.

The story is then picked up by my grandmother. She received letters from Raymond that were full of frustration. Grandma told me that Raymond would buy things for Mona and me, and then would come home to find that Pauline had sold them to get money. According to my grandmother, my mother was out partying more than she was home mothering, and, sure enough, she ended up pregnant again when Mona was only three months old. My mother tells a different story of her very jealous husband who locked her up whenever he left to go to work. I believe the truth more than likely lies somewhere between these two stories.

I am not totally sure what transpired during this time, but somehow my mother ended up back in Belleville, Ontario, where the Children's Aid stepped in and took custody of Mona and me. Mona was placed in the hospital, because she was sick and suffering from malnourishment, and I have no idea where I was during this period. The baby that Pauline was pregnant with at that time was a boy, and he was immediately given up for adoption when he was born. From the Children's Aid report that I have, this third child was adopted a few months later, and to this day I have no idea where he is. I have registered with Belleville Children's Aid in semi-hopes of finding him. You will see why I say "semi" hopes later on, but for now I turn my story to my experiences and perceptions.

Chapter 2
The Early Years

My earliest memory, or at least I believe it is a memory, is of sitting on a floor eating eggs out of a frying pan. Somewhere in the background, Mona, my baby sister, is crying in her crib. Now, this may be a pseudo memory from stories that I heard during the years when I was growing up, but it just feels like a real memory. I must have been less than eighteen months old, because by the time I was a year and a half, Mona and I were in the custody of Children's Aid and placed in a foster home at the Mastersons'.

The Masterson family, which became Mona's and my true family lived on a second-generation family farm with a huge old farmhouse and three generations of Mastersons filling the rooms. The farmhouse was a center-hall plan, two-story white wooden frame house with a veranda running along the front and down one side. As you went in through the front door, there was a staircase directly in front of you. To the left was the parlor, and to the right was the front room or winter kitchen. At the back, behind the staircase, was a bedroom, and a huge closet ran all the way across the back of the parlor. If you went to the right through the front room, you would enter a pantry where all of the food was kept, and there was a big cast-iron sink with a cistern and pump that pumped rainwater up from the cellar. Beyond the pantry was the summer kitchen, and behind the summer kitchen there was an attached woodshed and indoor outhouse. The parlor had a potbellied wood stove in the center of the room, while the summer and winter kitchen each had their own wood-burning cookstove.

Upstairs was a long hallway that led out to a veranda at the front and two bedrooms off each side. The basement steps were located under the main staircase and led to a cellar with dirt floors and stone-block walls. The cellar was divided into different areas, with the cistern on one side and huge bins built on the other side to store potatoes, apples, and other vegetables that were grown in the garden out back. The wall that faced the bottom of the stairs had large pickle barrels on the floor and shelves that held all of the canned fruits and vegetables.

Outside there was a front yard with a well and pump that was used to provide drinking water for the house and a side yard that led out to the garden and further on to the barn. A laneway also ran along the side yard out to the barn where the animals were housed. Across the driveway from the house was the "drive house," where the car and tractor was stored, and, if you went down the laneway toward the barn, there was a long building on the left that housed the chicken coop on one end and the pigpen on the other.

Francis, the youngest son of twelve children, had taken over the farm from his parents and was the man I would come to know as Daddy. He became a father who, even now, forty years after his death, I continue to admire and idolize.

When Mona and I first came to the farm, I have been told that he (from now on known as Daddy) did not want us to stay. He was looking for strapping young men who could help on the farm, not a five-month-old and an eighteen-month-old—and girls to boot. However, he was outvoted by others in the family, and Mona and I got to stay. I think that in retaliation for being overruled, he had the final say by renaming us. He immediately gave us boys' names, which somehow stuck, and all during our growing up years I was known as "John" and Mona's nickname was "Bill."

Mona was fresh out of the hospital and required much tender, loving care, while I, being the tough and independent one, even then just seemed to go along with whatever life was offering. This set the tone for our childhood, and my sense of independence and self-determination increased. As I grew older, I become increasingly convinced that I was the wild, difficult one and that Mona was the meek and favored one, and, to my way of thinking, she always got what she wanted. To this day, Mona will dispute this claim, and she sees her early life in much different circumstances. Her perspective is somewhat of a contrast to mine, and that's okay with me, because I truly believe that we all see things from our own viewpoints and it's not possible for two people to perceive situations in identical ways.

We were opposite in many ways. In 1958 Mona and I were given IQ tests, and it was determined by someone that I "displayed commendable intellectual versatility and special verbal powers" and would not have to work hard to learn, whereas Mona, although also smart, would have to work to achieve high marks. Talk about self-fulfilling prophesies! Hearing this as I grew up, I had the idea that I could learn very easily, and consequently I never bothered to study. As a result, I did okay, and I graduated high school with a 78 percent average three weeks after my seventeenth birthday. I didn't have a clue how to study. Mona, on the other hand, studied for hours each evening and never seemed to be content to get less than a high 90 percent average.

None of this really had any impact on me until I went back to school at forty-three years of age. I was in college (better late than never) and had no idea how to study. As with everything else, I flubbed my way through and finally came to realize that my most productive learning time was very early in the morning and that I could learn more by attending class and listening than by studying a book. I am a visual person and can close my eyes and recall conversations and information by imagining the person teaching the lesson and their body language, along with any visuals provided and the questions asked by others in class. I guess this worked pretty well for me, because I graduated on the dean's list a few years later at the age of forty-eight.

Moving back into some sort of chronological order here, apparently, when I first came to the farm, I had never seen a man without a suit and tie, and I was terrified of going near Daddy in his plaid shirt and farmer pants until that first Sunday, when he changed his clothes and put on his suit for church. Once he was all dressed up, I immediately went to sit on his lap and became his shadow from that day forward.

As for the rest of the family, I don't really remember my first impressions of them, except that there were a lot of them. Betty, at six years old, was the next closest in age to Monie, as we most times called her, and me. I don't think she was entirely happy being usurped as the baby of the family, and I can't say that I blame her. Next, there was Carl, who was nine, and then Helen, who would have been eleven. Following Helen was Lois at fourteen, Barb, around twenty, I think, and then Joe and Gerry who were already grown up and married when Mona and I came along. These were the biological children of the Mastersons, but over the years there were additional foster kids or godchildren. There was Reg, who is the same age as Lois and has been in the family for as long as I can remember, and somewhere along the line three of his brothers were tied in with the family. Later on there was Buster, who was Ma and Daddy's godchild, and Terry, another foster child. They were in their early teens when they came into the family and were around the same age as Carl.

With a family this large, there was never a shortage of playmates. Learning to get along and knowing that even if you disagree with someone you can learn to work it out and move on is a wonderful lesson. Many brief relationships occur because people never learned how to do this, and as soon as they realize someone is not "perfect," they move on to the next relationship. I have seen this happen in romantic relationships as well as friendships, and I think it's a real shame because these people miss out on some great opportunities for growth. Okay, okay, that's my sermon for this chapter!

I was one of those kids that you could bath and dress up and as soon as you could turn your back I would be mussed and dirty. I loved the fields and the barn and from an early age would spend much of my time in these places. We did not have hydro, therefore no television, but I do not ever remember being bored. I spent the first nine years of my life learning to milk cows and to drive a tractor and an old 1949 Dodge truck. When I wasn't doing chores, I was walking in the woods or sitting in a big tree and reading a book or thinking up new tricks to torment Mona with. In hindsight, I can see that I was oftentimes mean to Monie, and I really don't know why I did many of the things that I did. Maybe I was jealous of her, or perhaps I was paying back some of the crap that I felt that I was getting from my sister Betty, who had been the baby of the family until Mona and I came along.

Chapter 3
Using My Imagination

As I think back to those earlier times, poor Mona was subjected to an awful lot of childhood torment, including me telling her scary stories when we went to bed at night. Because she and I were so much younger, we were always the first ones to be put to bed. We slept together in a big, old double bed in one of the four bedrooms upstairs. We knew the bed was old because it sagged in the middle, and we were constantly rolling into each other at night. Because we had no hydro, quite a few months of the year it was dark when we went to bed, and the only light was a coal oil lamp on a table at the top of the stairs in the hallway. When we went to bed, I would make up stories of how a wicked witch was hiding in the closet and was going to come out during the night and steal Monie away, or whatever other frightening tales I could think up. I was constantly playing dirty tricks on her, and one time I even put poop on my finger and told her it was peanut butter. Somehow, she didn't buy that story.

Another time, she got a new sweater and I didn't, so I threw hers down the toilet hole in our winter outhouse. That was the indoor outhouse that was attached to the woodshed at the back of the house. We were only allowed to use it in the cold winter months, so we didn't have to go outside and freeze our butts off (literally).

Even when I tried to be helpful to Monie, I still got into trouble. One time, when we were about four and five years old, we were in bed, and Monie had to go to the bathroom. Now this wasn't a big deal, because there was a chamber pot in the hallway to use at night. The trouble was, she had to go number two, and that was not allowed in the chamber pail. We knew that if we crept downstairs, we would get into trouble, so we had a dilemma. Then I came up with the perfect plan! Monie would go in the pot, and then we would carry it into Daddy's room and throw it out his bedroom window. It would roll down the roof, off the back verandah, and land harmlessly in the backyard. If anyone saw it, he or she would just think that the dog had done it. Everything went exactly as planned until we threw the contents of the chamber pail out the window. Can you believe it—Uncle Fred, who was visiting, just happened to be coming in from the barn—and guess what? Sure enough it landed right on his head! Monie and I heard a huge roar (Uncle Fred was a big man), and I don't think that either of our feet even touched the floor as we ran back to the safety of our room. Our little hearts were jumping right out of our chests as we flew into bed and pulled the covers up over our heads, but, when someone was sent up to get us, I guess the shaking of the blankets was a dead giveaway that we were not asleep. We were both hauled downstairs unceremoniously and had to wash Uncle Fred's head. Thank goodness he was almost bald! Needless to say, we never tried that particular trick again!

There were times when Monie and I got along really well, and, between the two of us, we had the best imagination ever! We played house a lot, and we had to have a husband, so we would compete for the coveted stovepipe that ran from the woodstove downstairs, up through the floor in the center of the room. Whichever one of us was successful got to put a necktie around the stovepipe and pretend that it was our husband. We also practiced kissing our husband whenever the stovepipe wasn't too hot.

If we were outside, we would ride the old gas tank that Daddy used to fill up the tractor with gas. We would pretend it was our own special horse that could take us on journeys to magical places. Once, Carl thought he would give us a treat by letting us ride on one of the real horses that we had. He was leading the horse with Monie and me on her back when a bee stung the horse on the rump. The horse reared, and Monie and I both went flying into the dirt. I landed on top of poor

Monie. Fortunately, neither of us was hurt beyond a few scrapes, but, from then on, we preferred the gas tank.

We kept ourselves amused with all kinds of things. We used to go into the woods and collect burrs from the burdock weeds in the summertime, and we would stick them together and make all kinds of things. One of our favorite things to make was baskets or purses. If you were careful, you could put berries or pretend money (leaves from trees) or anything else you could think of that wasn't too heavy in your basket.

One day, when I was about four years old, the whole family came home from church on Sunday, and Monie and I stayed out to play in the yard until lunch was ready. Monie found something strange that we had never seen before, and, after we had cautiously examined it, we asked what it was. Daddy told us that it was a milk snake that someone in the family had killed the night before. He then told Carl to get rid of it. Carl carefully picked it up using the handle of a pitchfork. He had that dead snake precariously balanced over that fork handle and turned to fling it out into the orchard. As he did this, that snake slipped right off that handle and ended up wrapped around my leg, scaring the living daylights right out of me. I don't remember anything else about the incident, but I do know that I was petrified of snakes from that moment on. Some forty years later, I finally confronted that fear in a hypnosis session, and it took me right on back to a totally different life. I will relate that story when I get to that time in my life.

Chapter 4
Disappointment and Death × 2

In our family, with Mona and I, there were six girls. I don't remember my oldest sister, Barb, getting married, but I do remember that when she got married she moved to Chalk River with her husband, Bernard. Ma and Daddy used to visit her occasionally, and for some reason Monie always got to go with them but I had to stay behind at Aunt Rita's house. I do, however, vividly remember Barb moving back home again. She hadn't been married very long when she went to the doctor thinking she was pregnant. Instead, the doctor told her she had cancer. As was the custom in those days, she moved back home to be with her family. The house was rearranged, and a bed was brought down to the parlor. This room became Barb's room until she died two years later at the age of twenty-four. I remember vaguely what it was like in the parlor during the time that she was sick. There were candles burning seemingly all the time, and it also appeared that someone was always saying prayers or the rosary. Mona and I weren't allowed in very often, but, during one of the times that we were permitted in, Barb told me that when she got better she was going to buy me a new Easter hat. I thought that was a pretty good thing.

It was a hot August day when she died. Betty had Monie and me in the car, in the drive house. We were playing "car," and Betty was the mom in the front seat driving. Monie and I were her kids, and we had to sit in the backseat. Betty was pretending to drive us all over the place, shopping and visiting, and Monie and I were being held "play hostages," because we really hadn't wanted to play. All of a sudden we heard crying and carrying on in the yard, and we heard Lois say she was going to throw her rosary beads over the barn. Betty said, "Barb's dead," and took off into the house, leaving Monie and me in the car.

I was very upset with Barb, because I had no idea of what "dead" was, but I was pretty sure it meant that she was never going to get me the new hat that she had promised me. Isn't it interesting, the strange little details that go through your head at times like this?

As was the custom at the time, the parlor was put back together, and the bed was replaced with a casket, for Barb's three-day wake. The house was full of people, and there was so much food that you could have fed an army. My first experience with a death did not seem scary or even all that strange. Life went on as usual, and my six-year-old mind accepted death as just another aspect of life. I guess that was a good thing, because a mere five months later there was another death in the family—and this time it would be much more significant.

The second death was quite different and very sudden. We were all at school, which consisted of one room with all eight grades and a grand total of sixteen kids. It was January 26, and Mrs. Cassidy, our teacher, was sitting at a desk eating a can of sardines. While she was eating, Don Baldrick, Ma and Daddy's best friend, stopped in and spoke with her. She got my sister Betty, who was in grade seven, and my cousin Anne. They both left with Don, and, although, this was extremely unusual, my six-year-old mind didn't think much of it. At the end of the day, Don came once again to the school, this time to pick up Monie and me. I still did not think something was wrong; we just happy not to have that long walk home. When we got home, the house was full of people, and no one was paying any attention to us. Even in those days, it was typical for me to try to remain invisible when there were a bunch of people around, so I just sat on a chair in the front room and tried to get my winter boots and snow leggings off all by myself. There was usually one of the older kids around to help us, but this time I was on my own because everyone else seemed busy doing other things. I was having quite a struggle, and, in the middle of trying to get my winter clothing off, Grandma Masterson came over to me and said, "Have you no shame, girl! Your mother dead and you don't even shed a tear." And that's how I found out Ma died. I immediately started crying, because that's what I thought I was supposed to do, and from that moment forward, I think I subconsciously added another person

(Grandma Masterson) to my list of people that I either didn't like or was angry with because I sensed their disapproval of me.

I later learned that Ma had been cleaning out the milk pails and stood up and said to Daddy, "Francis, I have an awful pain in my head," and she died standing right there. Once again, there was a coffin in the parlor and a three-day wake. Daddy took over the role of both mother and father and, to my young mind, life continued on in a normal fashion, while at the same time being completely different. Although I didn't realize it at the time, the difference would mean almost complete freedom while I was growing up.

Just to backtrack a little bit, there were a few notable incidents that involved Ma that I remember.

The first memory was from a few years earlier, and it was before I started school. I remember Monie and me sitting on the floor in the front room, and Ma was lying on the couch. To this day I don't know if we were being noisy and Ma was trying to scare us into being quiet or if she was trying to entertain us. All I know is that somehow she got our attention, and, when we looked at her there on the couch, she stuck out her false teeth at us. Well, I had never seen anything like that before, and it immediately scared me into being quiet. I was really quite leery of her after that.

Another time, for some reason, I took a crayon and decided to draw on the wall coming down the stairs. When Ma saw it, needless to say, someone was in deep trouble. But the nice thing about being one of the youngest in a large family is there is always someone there to stick up for you or to try to protect you. While Ma was trying to get to me, probably to give me a spanking, Helen, my older sister, kept me behind her back and told Ma that she had been the one to mark on the walls. Imagine that! She must have been about fourteen at the time, and far beyond the age of scribbling on walls, but, nevertheless, she insisted and eventually Ma let it go. I never did get punished for it.

The last significant memory of Ma happened on a Friday night shortly before she died. It was a regular occurrence on Friday nights to go into town to pick up groceries and to meet my oldest sister, Lois, when she got off the bus at Mrs. Blakely's bakery. Lois worked and boarded twenty-three miles away in Belleville during the week and would take the bus home for the weekend every Friday night.

I loved going into Mrs. Blakely's bakery and waiting for the bus to bring Lois home. There were always fresh-baked cinnamon buns sitting on the counter, and the place smelled like I imagine Heaven must smell with fresh-baked bread and all kinds of goodies. In the back was a big empty room with wide-plank flooring and wooden benches along the walls. This was where travelers waited for their bus. Anyway, on this particular Friday night, Daddy loaded Betty, Monie, and me into the car in the drive house and then pulled the car around to pick up Ma. We drove up, and there was Ma, looking up into the sky and acting like she was talking to someone and then she gave a wave toward the sky. Daddy, becoming somewhat impatient, said, "Come on, Lizzie, get in the car and stop that foolishness." Ma got into the car and said that she had been talking to Barb and that Barb had told her that she would see her soon. Daddy mumbled something about her foolishness, and then, to my knowledge, the subject was dropped and nothing more was said about it. Shortly thereafter, sure enough, Ma went to meet up with Barb in Heaven. Although, at six years old, I did not really understand what was going on, this scene stayed with me and came back to haunt me some thirty-one years later when my husband, Bruce, announced that our deceased son, Brad, had paid him a visit.

This last story of Ma conflicts somewhat with the memory of some other family members, and I did not know about this until forty-six years later. While relating this story at the time of my brother-in-law's death, my sister Helen said that it did not happen that way at all and that Ma had been standing at the back door of the big house when it happened. I think, other than where it happened, the memory of the family members was otherwise the same.

Chapter 5
Getting Our Religious Education

My growing up years also had many happy memories. Sunday was a new day for a new week, and it seemed like every Saturday was preparation for this new beginning. The whole family was involved in cleaning the house from top to bottom, shining our good shoes for church, and having our weekly bath in a stainless steel washtub. Because we didn't have running water, the washtub would be brought into the front room, and we would heat water on top of the woodstove to fill it. One of the best things about being one of the youngest was that I got to bathe first. I always figured that Monie and I got to bathe when the water was nice and clean because little people weren't as dirty as the bigger people. I can't imagine what the water looked like after everybody had washed. While Ma was still alive, she would line us up after our bath and give each one of us a chocolate square. I never figured out why Betty always ran around behind the stove and spit hers out into the wood box. Now I know that it was because she was giving us an ex-lax to make sure we went to the bathroom! With so many kids, it would have been difficult to check each of us on a regular basis, so I guess it was easier this way.

On Saturdays the floor in the front room, also referred to as the winter kitchen, was waxed. This was a lot of fun for Monie and I. I know, you're wondering how waxing the floor can be fun. Well, let me tell you. The older kids usually did all the work, and in those days the floors were waxed with paste wax. They would spread the wax all over the floor, wait for it to dry, and then polish it off. We didn't have hydro, so the polishing had to be done manually, which meant taking an old blanket and pulling it across the floor. The blanket worked better with weight on it, and this is where Monie and I came in handy. We were small enough to be pulled around on the blankets, and we found it so much fun, that I think the floor got 'super polished'. We would fly around the room on our "magic carpets," pulled by Carl or Helen or one of the older siblings. It was great fun.

Carl always found new ways to keep us entertained too. He would use an old blanket and play Mother Hen with us or teach us how to do somersaults using his knees as a springboard. He tried to teach us how to dance sort of Hungarian-style—squatting on the floor with our arms crossed and kicking our legs out. I don't think we were very successful with that one, or at least I wasn't because I've always been a little deficient with my coordination. He was also responsible for teaching us to jive a few years later.

As the older sisters and brothers grew up and finished their education, they either went to Belleville to find a job or helped Daddy work the farm. Those who worked away from home used to come home on weekends, and, after we had hydro installed, it was rare for them to come home without a new forty-five or LP (record) that had just come out. We would play the new records almost nonstop, and I still remember almost every word of those songs by heart. I even remember the words to some of the songs that were on the back of the records but never made it to the hit parade.

One Friday night when Lois came home on the bus, we met her at Mrs. Blakely's, and she decided to get us a treat. We walked over to Kwans, the only Chinese restaurant in town, and Lois ordered us some french fries. I hadn't heard her place the order, and, because I had never had french fries before, I thought they were pretty special. I heard someone else order *fishin chips* for their meal, and, when they got their order, there were french fries on his plate. I just assumed that the fries were called *fishin chips*, so the next time Lois took us to Kwans, I asked for fishin chips. Lois said that I just wanted chips. I was upset because I thought chips meant plain, old potato chips, but, lo and behold, when our order came, there on the plate were the french fries that I had so badly wanted. This was a good lesson in trust, because it was incidents like this that made me want to be a good person for Lois. I often heard her say, "I don't have any problem with John. Whenever I ask her do something, she does it for me." Well, that's probably because she asked and gave me a choice. It seemed like everybody else just told me what to do.

Before we had hydro, we would entertain ourselves on Saturday afternoons with an old, windup Victrola that was in the upstairs hallway. We were supposed to be cleaning, but somehow we found time to put on seventy-eight records and pretend it was the olden days. We would poke fun at the songs and make up silly dances, pretending to be Ma and Daddy when they were dating.

On many Saturday nights we kneeled around the front room and said the rosary. I don't remember if we did that every week or only sometimes, but I do know that it was important to say our prayers every night. The first time that I forgot to say my prayers, I was about six years old. I woke up in the middle of the night, and I realized that I hadn't said my prayers. I was so scared that I couldn't get out of that bed fast enough. I was sure that the devil was on my heels, ready to steal me away to hell. I don't think that I've ever said my prayers as fast as I did that night! And honestly, I don't think that I ever forgot to say them again for a long, long time, probably until after I was married.

As good Catholics, we regularly went to confession on Saturday afternoon or early Sunday morning before Mass. From the time I made my first confession until I was in my teens, my confession never changed. Every week I confessed to the same sins so that I could go to Communion on Sunday, and then, as soon as church was over, I felt free to start racking up those same old sins all over again, so I'd have something to confess to the next week. The weekly ritual was "Bless me, Father, for I have sinned. I lied, I swore, and I fought with my sisters." The penance would always be the same too. It was one Our Father and ten Hail Marys.

A lot of things in our life were connected to prayers and the church. We used to go to Mass on Sunday morning, and then the kids would stay behind and have catechism lessons for another hour, while the adults socialized and gossiped about each other outside. We had one aunt, Norma, who used to chase us around and ask for a hug. We were a bit leery of her because she was so different from our other aunts, who were prim and proper. Aunt Norma used to give us humbugs out of her purse. We took them because we didn't want to be impolite, but we rarely ate them because they were usually coated in layers of lint from the depths of her purse. Her purse was full of all kinds of things, and we never knew what else might be attached to those humbugs!

One time on our way to church, I was mad at Monie for something or other and decided to get even with her. I found one of those brown and orange striped wooly caterpillars crawling around outside and brought it into church with me. While Monie was being prim and proper, kneeling with her head bowed and saying her prayers, I casually dropped the caterpillar down the back of her dress. If you've ever had one of these things land on you, you know that they throw hairs or something when they're frightened. I thought it was pretty funny at the time, watching Monie squirm around and make quite a scene, but, when all was said and done, as usual I was in deep doo-doo.

Prayers also figured into our punishments at home when we misbehaved. One August, I got a new pair of shoes for going back to school. I wasn't supposed to be wearing them but had managed to sneak them on and get out of the house without being seen. I'm not sure where I was going or where I had been, but somehow Betty saw me and said that she was going to tell on me for wearing my new shoes. I knew that I was more than likely in trouble, because Betty usually enjoyed telling on me, so I let her go on ahead and I took the longest time that I could going home. I was so mad at her that I was kicking the shoes off and flinging them with my feet ahead of me. I flung a little too hard, and that darn shoe went flying into the creek that ran along the side of the road. Now I was really in big trouble! Not only had I worn the new shoes, but I had ruined one by getting it all wet. I did my best to sneak home without getting caught, thinking that if the shoe dried out, then maybe that part of my sin would never be discovered. But, as usual, I got caught. Daddy was working in the front yard, in the process of installing an old wooden barrel to make a flowerbed. He had both ends out of the barrel but didn't have any soil in it yet, and, being the enterprising father that he was, he promptly made me crawl through the barrel on my hands and knees twenty five times, saying an Our Father and Hail Mary out loud each time I went through. To top things off, Betty was sitting on the upstairs verandah, where she had a perfect view of my total humiliation.

Daddy didn't believe in hitting his kids. Instead, he would punish us in a way that we wouldn't forget about anytime soon. I think that his way was probably a lot more effective than a spanking. Almost fifty years later, I can remember those punishments as if they were yesterday, and spankings probably would not have been quite as memorable.

I do have to tell you though, that he did spank me once. I had pushed him beyond his limits, and he really didn't know what else to do with me. It happened early one morning when I was about eleven. The big house had burned down, and we were living in the little house. I used to get up and start the fire in the morning, and then Betty would come out by the stove where it was warm and get dressed in comfort. I don't know why, but I used to hate it when she did this. We would usually fight. Well, this one day, we started fighting, and I happened to have a butcher knife in my hand. I was so mad that I threw it at her. As soon as I did that, I knew I had done something really, really bad and was in big trouble again, so I headed out the back door. I heard someone behind me, and, assuming it was Betty coming after me, I grabbed one of those heavy, green-glass pop bottles, not the plastic ones like we have today. As she came through the door, I hit her over the head with it. As soon as this happened, I saw that it wasn't Betty at all, but poor Monie, who was completely innocent in all of this. Then I really got scared and ran up the road to go hide. I didn't get far, because Daddy was just coming down the road from the barn, and he must have heard all the screaming and yelling. When he saw me running, I guess he just knew I was in trouble again. I ran right into him. He grabbed me by the arm and said, "John, this time, you've run into the hands of the law!" and then he gave me a few smacks on my ass. I was so shocked that he had actually hit me that I just stood there and peed in my pants. The spanking didn't hurt at all, because I don't actually think he hit me that hard, but the fact that he spanked me meant that he was really, really, really mad and that scared me more than anything.

In retrospect, I probably thought that the spanking meant that there was a chance that maybe he could send me back to Children's Aid or something. I don't know why I thought that he might send me back. He never actually said anything to that effect, but sometimes, when I didn't want to do something that needed to be done, he would say, "I paid eighty-five dollars for you, now, you damn well do as I say." It was never said with malice or as a threat, just as a statement of fact. I don't ever remember taking offense, but somehow, in the back of my mind, there must have been the ghost of a fear instilled that he could return me for a refund!

Some of the other family members had different ideas about punishment, and Helen was the worst that I remember. If Monie and I were fighting, she would make us sit on chairs side by side with our arms around each other. Yuk! Sometimes, if we got off lucky, she would put us each on a chair on either side of the fridge and make us sit there and be quiet for twenty minutes. This punishment wasn't quite so bad, because, when she wasn't looking, Monie and I would make faces at each other behind the fridge.

For some unknown reason, I used to wet the bed on a regular basis. I slept in a crib until I was at least four or five years old and was thoroughly toilet trained. I remember sitting up in my crib and thinking that I was on the chamber pail, and, as soon as I started to go to the bathroom, I would wake up. One day, when Ma and Daddy were out, this happened and I guess Helen decided that she would do something about it. She hauled me downstairs to the pantry and put me up on a chair in front of the sink. She made me wash my own urine-soaked clothes. I never have liked washing in cold water, and having to do my own laundry in the cold water from the cistern must have been the catalyst that I needed for change because I never wet the bed after that day. I guess Helen was getting her mothering practice for the four kids of her own that she would have someday.

Chapter 6
The Truth Hurts

Having Betty as the next oldest sister often meant being educated much more quickly than I probably would have been otherwise. I understand now that it was sibling rivalry at its finest, but, at the time, it really didn't seem like a whole lot of fun. Whenever Betty learned something new, she made sure Monie and I were aware of it too. Like the time she found out there was no such thing as Santa Claus. We didn't believe her and told her she was lying, at which point she promptly took us to the sideboard in the front room and showed us what we were getting for Christmas. She also made us stay up after midnight Mass on Christmas Eve and peek over the railing so that we could see that it was just my brother Joe, with bells in his hands and saying, "Ho, ho, ho," and then going into the parlor and pretending to put our presents under the tree. Sure enough, Christmas morning, there under the tree were the things that she had showed us. I can't really remember the details of the tooth fairy and the Easter bunny, but I'm sure they were similar situations.

Another time, she was mad at us for something or other and told us that we didn't belong there—we were just adopted and not really family. When we challenged her on this one, she once again took us to the sideboard and showed us a whole bunch of papers. Although, we were not old enough to read, we took her word for it, but I think that our young minds did not process the general idea of not belonging. She was just our mean sister, doing what most older sisters do.

The other learning moment that jumps out at me was a few years later when I was about eleven or twelve. Betty had just found out how babies were made and couldn't wait to impart this mind-boggling piece of information. We were in the barn, milking, just the two of us, and she told me in a very forthright manner. As this point, I think I still believed babies came from the cabbage patch, and something like this had never occurred to me. I was so shocked that I almost fell off my milking stool!

It seemed Betty was almost always available to catch my sins. If I got into trouble at school and had to stay after class, she often flew home to tell the story of my sins. There were even times when I hadn't done anything wrong that she could find a way to make it look like I had. One time I saw her and our cousin Anne steal one of Ma's cigarettes and head across the road and into the field. I followed them to see what they were doing, and there they were—sitting behind this big rock puffing away. When I said I was going to tell on them, they bribed me into not telling by allowing me to have a few puffs too, so I never did get to tattle on them. We now sit back and can laugh about these stories, and I think that having lived through all this has made us the interesting and unique family that we are.

Following Ma's death when I was six, things around the farm went on pretty much the same for the next few years. Lois, although working in Belleville through the week, would come home every Friday night and took over the mothering role, teaching us how to bake and buying us school clothes and necessities out of her own paycheck. She loved to shop and spoiled herself somewhat, but was always generous with her money, and I think she enjoyed shopping for us as much as for herself. She seemed so sophisticated with her nice clothes, and she even had three fur coats.

I was complacent with life on the farm and took to the country life pretty well. I was more than content to be out in the fields or the barn and was always ready to try something new. One of the things that I was keen on and thought would make me seem like a grown-up was milking the cows. I had watched all the others milking the cows every morning and night and figured that I should be able to do this too as a pretty, grown-up six-year-old. Daddy hadn't really encouraged me too much, so I took the initiative myself, watched how it was done for awhile and then figured that I could do it on my own. I had failed to notice that the milkers always sat on the same side of the cow. I grabbed a stool and a pail and moved in. I sat down and reached out to start milking. Well, let me tell you, that cow was not impressed with me coming in on the wrong side to get milk. Before I knew what was happening, I was on my backside in the drop, which is the trough that runs behind the cows, and you can imagine what it's used for. As it wasn't a bath night, I had to wash in cold water to get the smell off. After that, Daddy told me that, if I was going to milk the cows, he would show me how to do it properly. From that time on, I was in the barn twice a day, doing my share of the milking.

I also learned how to drive a tractor when I was about six. At this young age, I didn't have much muscle power to do any of the heavy stuff, and, by being able to drive the tractor, I freed up one of the boys who did have the strength. During the summer months, I would drive the tractor while someone else was on the wagon piling the hay that was being drawn in for the barn. I also did my time picking stones in the field and loading them on the stone boat so that the field would be ready for planting.

One of the most fun things that we did was jump in the haymows. Anyone who has ever experienced farm life can remember the joy of climbing high up to the top of the barn and jumping from the highest beam down onto mountains of fresh hay. There was enough room on the way down to do somersaults and all kinds of antics. Landing in the hay was like jumping into a cloud. Of course, we could only do this for the first while after the hay was brought in and was nice and soft. Later on, it would be packed down or half used up by the cows, and then one could get hurt.

We also had one mow that was straw, which was the chaff that the threshing machine created when it separated the oats from the plant for the animals to eat during the winter. The straw was used primarily for the cows to lie on and for the drop to absorb the cows' waste. The straw in the mow was as light as a feather but wasn't much fun because it got into your clothes and scratched the hell out of you—sort of like jumping into a bale of fiberglass insulation. And besides, it had an awful lot of dust with it. Consequently, we hardly ever played there.

Chapter 7
Neighborly Times

Life was pretty good on the farm. Although there were chores, I hardly remember ever questioning that work had to be done. We had a lot of freedom, and, even though we lived out of sight of our neighbors, Monie and I managed to fill our days with all kinds of things. We had what we called "the little house" just down the road. Ma and Daddy had built it when they got married and had later on moved up into what we called the big house. An old man named Archie lived in the little house, and we used to go down and visit him. He always had time for us when we went to visit and would listen to our stories. He also had lots of wine bottles around, and sometimes we would borrow an empty one when we needed another rolling pin while making pies or if Monie and I were playing house and making mud pies.

Another notable neighbor was Jenny Johnston. She lived in an old farmhouse down the road with her stepson, Leonard, who was almost as old as Daddy and had never gotten married. The house that they lived in was very old even then and was a long, two-story building with a veranda on the front. There was a front and back staircase, and you had to go through one room to get to the next room as there were no hallways. Their house had never been painted and was actually kind of spooky. Jenny Johnston was very old, or so it seemed to us, and stooped over when she walked. She was deaf and wore glasses that made her eyes look really big. But she was a kind enough old soul, and she used to let Monie and I go out into her orchard to pick apples because her apples were different from the ones we had in our orchard. She would also let us go upstairs and go through magazines, usually the *Family Herald*, whenever we had school projects to do. Monie and I used to love following behind her going up the stairs, because everybody said she had all kinds of money and that she kept it stuffed in the long stockings that she wore. We would follow behind her, trying to see under her dress to check out all the bulges in her legs, and. sure enough, it looked as though she really did keep her money there.

One day, when Monie and I went down to see Jenny, she let us out into the orchard, and, I guess because she was deaf, she didn't hear us come back in. When we came through the back door into the kitchen, there was Jenny Johnston lying on the couch. She had her glasses off, and her eyes were closed. It looked as though her eyes were sunk right through to the back of her head. Well, Monie and I thought she was dead, and we ran home as fast as our short, little legs would carry us. We ran until we found Daddy and started yelling at him that Jenny Johnston was dead. Daddy went straightaway to check on her and found that she had only been taking a nap! Even so, with death not being unusual to us and the fact that she was laying much the same way that Barb and Ma had been in their caskets, it was not a surprise for us to think that. Years later when we were in our early fifties, Mona and I had the opportunity to go back into that house. You'll hear about it later on, and the amazing thing was that the house was exactly as both of us remembered.

Another memory from this same neighbor occurred the day Betty and I decided that we needed to make some extra money for something that we wanted. For the life of me, I can't remember what we wanted to buy, but we approached Leonard Johnston and asked him if he had any chores that we could do. He told us that he would pay us six dollars if we stooked a field of grain for him. Now if you've ever seen a field of grain, farmers used to cut the grain and a machine would tie it into sheaves and spit them out around the field. You would then have to put five or six together and stand them up, making a tepee out of them. This way they could dry out and be ready for the threshing machine. This was called "stooking the grain." Well, Betty and I worked really hard and stooked that whole field. We were so proud of ourselves. We went the next day and collected our six dollars, and, to Leonard's credit, he never said a word about our work. What we found out later on was that we hadn't done the greatest job, and, without our knowing about it, Daddy had gone down in that field to check out our work and had

had to redo much of it so that Betty and I would get our money. Talk about a great dad!

We used to cut across Leonard's property to get down to the river to play. Although we couldn't swim very well, we liked to go there and dog-paddle out to a raft that one of the cottagers had anchored a little ways off shore. We weren't supposed to go down there, because Ma had been afraid of the water. I guess she was worried that one of us would drown. We were still told this even after Ma had died, but some of us would go there anyway to cool off in the summer. One time when Betty and Monie and I were down there, we dog-paddled out to the raft and got up on it and were just goofing around. Somebody spotted a black snake swimming in the water. Talk about scared silly. Here we were, stuck on a raft with a snake just swimming around and around us. I don't know how long we sat there, but we waited until it was long gone before we scrambled into the water and made our way to shore as fast as we could. Somehow, the lure of the cool water on hot summer days overrode my fear of seeing a snake. The incident didn't really dampen our spirits for swimming at all.

A few years later when I was nine years old, we finally got hydro. We had a television set, a fridge, and an electric wringer washer and a washtub for washing our clothes. At this time, Betty was the oldest one home, so she was kind of the boss of Monie and me. We three girls were home alone, because Daddy was out digging a grave for his brother, Uncle Fred (yes, the same one with poop on his head), who had died the day before and would be buried following his three day wake. The rest of the boys were out threshing at another farm. At that time, one farmer owned the thrashing machine, and all the farmers in the area would take turns going to each farm to help bring in the crops for winter. On this day in August, we were doing the laundry because Monie and I were going to go on a holiday in Belleville for a few days to stay with Aunt Leona, Daddy's sister.

There was a big, long closet that ran along the back of the parlor and under the stairs. In this closet were boxes and boxes of clothing that had been worn by all the children in various stages of their growth. I had gone into the closet to look for some clothes that might be good to go on holiday with, and I had taken a candle in so I could see because there was no hydro in this area. To this day, I am not sure what happened, because there was also a plug-in on the parlor wall near the closet that was exposed and had bare wires sticking out.

A little while after I had been in the closet, we were in the back kitchen doing laundry, and we smelled smoke. Betty noticed that the house was on fire and ran through to the front room to call the operator to try to get help. Then we ran through the back kitchen and out the back door. As we were leaving through the back of the house, Betty grabbed the radio off the shelf and got Monie and me outside. When we went out the back door, it locked behind us, and we couldn't get back into the house. Within minutes, the whole house was up in flames, and the three of us just stood there in shock.

A short time later, all the neighbors and thrashers came to help, but our only source of water was the well out front and it went dry very quickly. There was no fire department yet in Tweed, and the river was too far away to be of any help. So once the well went dry, there was nothing to do except watch the house burn. We lost everything except our lives and the radio in that fire. The house burned for three days, and the fire even cooked all the vegetables in the garden.

When the house burned, Monie and I hadn't even gotten dressed yet. We were wearing our new baby doll pajamas that Lois had bought for us because we were saving our clean clothes for going away. Besides that, we had gone down the road earlier in the morning to show old Archie our new pajamas.

There was so much confusion going on around the house burning down, and there were people everywhere. Somewhere in all the uproar, I thought about the candle that I had used in the back closet. As the realization of the situation sank in, I started yelling, "It's all my fault, I burned the house down!" Someone else mentioned the exposed hydro wires, but somehow, as the story unfolded in the family, that didn't carry much weight. Instead, "John burned the house down," was the most common explanation It became another sin to add to my ever-growing list.

When the big house burned down, we had no insurance, and, with the help of the Salvation Army, the Red Cross, and donations from the local residents, Daddy managed to fix up the little house that Archie had lived in. Betty stayed with our cousin Anne while Monie and I had to live with Ma's sister, Aunt Josephine, and her family while the little house was being fixed up, but shortly after the school year started we were back at home again.

The little house consisted of two rooms on the ground floor and a room upstairs that was only accessible by a ladder because there was no room for a staircase. One room downstairs had a wood stove and was a kitchen and living room combined, while the other room held two beds and a dresser. Upstairs, there was a double bed and a couple of single beds. Betty was there for the first while until she graduated high school and got a full-time job in Belleville. Then there was just Monie and me and Daddy left. All of the others still came home every weekend, and many weekends, there were so many of us that sometimes we slept three to a double bed!

Once again life carried on in a fairly normal fashion. I continued to get into trouble, and in some ways nothing much had changed. One thing that was different was that we had a creek running down behind the little house that was fun to play in. I know that water from the creek was perfectly good to drink, but we still had to go up the road to where the big house had been to get water from the well. Sometimes I got lazy, or shall we say creative, and I would take the pail down to the creek to fill it instead of making the long haul up the road to the well. One Sunday, my older brother Joe and his wife, Doreen, came for a visit. Doreen was a bit of a clean freak. She thought that our housekeeping skills were somewhat lacking, therefore she would never consider eating at our house. This one Sunday, she relented and said we could make her a cup of tea. Monie and I were sent up to get a pail of water. Instead of going all the way up to the well, we just went down to the creek, filled up the pail, and brought it back to the house. We filled the kettle, made a pot of tea, and then poured it into a cup for her. As she went to take a sip of her tea, there floating in her cup was a boiled pollywog. Needless to say, she didn't drink the tea. She was immediately ready to go home, where she could be assured of the water that she was drinking. Although I did get into trouble about it, the rest of the family certainly saw the humor in it. We all had a good laugh whenever the memory came up.

Chapter 8
School Encounters

That list of my sins was getting very long. Every year in public school, except for grades one and eight, I got the strap for something or another. The first time that I remember getting the strap was in grade two. One of the girls' moms had just had a baby, and it was the topic of conversation for the day. During our lunchtime, we were out behind the woodshed playing house. We had built "walls" in a rectangle by piling the wood around to a height of about two feet. I was the mother this time around while the others played various roles. I decided that, as the mother, I was going to have a baby. So I stuffed my over sweater under my regular sweater and was walking around like a pregnant mama, just as the teacher came walking around the side of the woodshed, probably to see what we were up to. She took one look at me and hauled me unceremoniously into the school to be introduced to the strap. Can you imagine? I guess she thought being pregnant was a sin!

Then, when I was going from grade four to grade five, I had somehow gotten the idea that passing from grade four made you grow boobs. Well, when September came and I still didn't have anything starting to grow there, I decided to take matters into my own hands, and I invented them by wearing a bra and stuffing it with Kleenex. Alvin, who was my archenemy throughout my public school years, started poking me in the chest and telling me they weren't real. He did this while we were lined up to wash our hands for lunch. I wasn't about to let him get away with that behavior, so I punched him pretty hard.

He was just a big sissy anyway, and, because he was about three years older than I, he should have been able to defend himself. He didn't, and, when he whined and tattled on me, I got the strap again!

Another time, one of the older girls gave me a fountain pen that she didn't want anymore. After she gave it to me, we got into a squabble, and she decided that I wasn't her friend. So she took it back and gave it to Alvin. A little later in the day, Alvin was using it on a piece of foolscap that he was doing his writing exam on and was gloating about having the pen. I made an excuse to go to the pencil sharpener and accidentally gave him a good elbow in the ribs on the way by. His pen went berserk across the page, and he once again squealed to the teacher. Sure enough, it was the strap for me once again. A few days later, I managed to get a hold of the fountain pen when he wasn't around, and I sharpened it in the pencil sharpener. If I couldn't have that pen, then he couldn't either. So that was the end of the fountain pen, but once again I got hauled in after school for the strap.

During the winter, the neighbor across the road from the school used to come over early and start the fire in the woodstove at school. We were at the school long before the teacher, because we had managed to get a ride on the school bus. We were left to our own devices until the teacher got there, and, because it was so cold, the school was unlocked early. Well, on one particular morning, Alvin and I were once again fighting like cats and dogs. He was down by the door, and I was up by the teacher's desk trying to avoid him. Because his words hurt the most, that was his weapon of choice. My retaliation was to throw a pair of scissors from the teacher's desk at him. Just as I whipped them as hard as I could at him, he ducked, and the teacher, who just happened to be coming through the door, ended up getting hit with them. Well, guess what? Sure enough, I got the strap again!

When I wasn't getting the strap, I was getting into trouble in other ways. Sometimes when the weather was good we would take a shortcut through the fields to school, and, in the spring, there were wild leeks that grew along the way. I have no idea why, but I loved weird things. Every spring I would pick the leeks and eat them on the way to school. I never noticed, but apparently everyone else did, because I smelled so bad that I would get sent home. Daddy always said that if you gave me a saltshaker and a garden, I would have lunch and be happy. I never worried about washing the food off. I guess I took that old saying to heart: "Everyone eats a peck of dirt before they die." Maybe doing that wasn't the best thing for me, but here I am still kicking and screaming my way through life. I have never had the flu, very rarely get a cold, and am generally very healthy.

One day as we were walking home from school, one of the other girls and I got into a fight. She made me so mad that I picked up a dead skunk off the road and threw it at her. I always seemed to get caught when I did something wrong, and this time was no exception. By the time the air got cleared with the parents over this incident, I was scared silly that I was going to have to have rabies shots. Betty took great pride in telling me that I might have to get twenty-eight needles in the stomach, or else I would get rabies, foam at the mouth, and start acting weird the way that some of the wild animals did every spring. Of course, the good news was that the skunk wasn't rabid and nothing happened, but I certainly did worry about having to go to a doctor and the other horrible things that Betty had told me would happen to me.

I got a scare one other time at school when I was about ten years old. I went out to the girls' outhouse to go to the bathroom. Something didn't feel right, and, in my investigation of what was going on, I discovered a big, fat worm coming out of me. Talk about being horrified! I never did tell anyone about it, because I would have been too embarrassed. But it was a very long time before I stopped checking to see if there were any more.

Other than the times when I got into trouble or received the strap, I really loved our little white clapboard, one-room school. I felt secure among the smells of books, chalk, and the wood burning in the big, pot-bellied stove in the middle of the room. It felt like a safe place to be, and I think that I must have at least partially begun developing my social skills. It was also here that I became aware that I was different. We were the only family without two parents, and, whether it was real or imagined, I always felt that I did not fit in. After all, not only did I only have one parent, but I was also one of the "adopted ones" in a community of family-oriented, God-fearing people! It seemed that Monie and I were always known as "those two that Lizzie and Francis took in," and then, about grade seven, we had a teacher who opened a whole new world for me.

Mrs. Genore was absolutely wonderful. I guess she felt that all of us "country bumpkins" could use a little culture. She had a son attending university in Ottawa, and, as was typical of any parent with a child away at school, she visited whenever she could. When we were in our final year of public school, she took the grade eight class, which consisted of Susan and me, to Ottawa on one of her visits to see her son. We spent the entire day seeing Capital Hill, the Parliament buildings, and a tour through one of the museums that was full of fascinating things, including totem poles that stretched three stories high and all kinds of historically significant displays.

I had never even dreamed that such wonderful things existed. From that day forward, I idolized this woman for opening my eyes to the enormous world that existed outside the boundaries of Tweed and Belleville. It certainly provided a yearning to see everything that the world had to offer. To this day, I love to travel and explore new places and to absorb the history of whichever area of the world I am visiting. My sense of foreign adventure began there in grade eight, and then not soon enough it was time to move on to high school.

Chapter 9
A Little Fish in the Big Pond

I was twelve years old and moving from a one-room school with sixteen kids to a huge school with indoor bathrooms, a different teacher for each class, and over two hundred kids. I was a little fish in a big pond, and I was hell-bent for election on making sure that I experienced everything that I possibly could! At Tweed High School, classes were divided according to where a student's name fell in the alphabet. My best friend up to grade 8 was now placed into a different classroom because her name fell at the end of the alphabet. Mine was in the middle, so little Dorothy Masterson got thrown into the grade 9B pond to fend for herself. But that was okay with me, because I really thought I was a big shot in a grown-up world. I took every opportunity that I could to fit in with what I considered to be the "in crowd." I made friends with a girl named Connie, and she introduced me to the world of smoking, boys, and skipping school. It wasn't that I hadn't been a handful in public school, but this was a whole new ball of wax. Not everyone knew who I was, so I got away with a lot more.

I think Connie appealed to me because she did all of the aforementioned things and was a non-Catholic to boot! We flirted with boys, skipped school, got our ears pierced, and did all kinds of things that we were not supposed to do. I really hadn't figured out the whole sex thing yet. I was pretty sure that you didn't do the thing to make babies until after you were married, and I thought that kissing and petting were considered pretty wild exploits. To my knowledge, Connie was of the same mind. Both of our families discouraged our relationship and did everything they could to keep us apart. But the more they discouraged it, the stronger the bond became, or so I thought.

Even some of my classmates tried to discourage our friendship. One day, Connie was not at school, and we were sitting in math class waiting for the teacher, Mr. English, to come in. Peter, one of my classmates, said to me, "You shouldn't be hanging around with her. She's a PT, you know." I asked him what a PT was, and he looked at me as if I was stupid. "A PT is a prostitute," he replied. I answered him with, "So what, she's a prostitute and I'm a Catholic, what's the big deal?" He then proceeded to explain to me what a prostitute was. To say the least, I was flabbergasted and decided to ask Connie about this as soon as I got a chance. She was at school the next day, and we decided to skip and go down by the railway tracks. I asked her about it. She told me it was all lies and that she had been raped when she was thirteen. Because she was no longer a virgin, all the guys had labeled her as easy. She cried when she told me the story, and I firmly believed every word she said, which only made me more determined to be her friend!

Things changed in my home life shortly after that and we drifted apart, but I continued to defend her at every opportunity until I moved to Oshawa for grade eleven. One day, shortly after I moved to Oshawa, I was coming home on the bus and there was Connie, about eight months pregnant. She barely acknowledged my existence. This was my first major betrayal and my first lesson in putting my trust in anyone who called themselves my friend. I now know that there may have been extenuating circumstances surrounding her pregnancy and that I shouldn't have made such a harsh judgment, but I was barely fifteen years old and did not have the life skills to work that out yet.

During this time Daddy discovered a pack of smokes in my coat pocket one night. I did what every kid through the ages has done in this circumstance and told him that they weren't mine. I told him I was keeping them for a friend so her parents wouldn't find out she smoked. For the first time, he believed me and told me to give them back to her and not to do that anymore. Relieved at being let off the hook so easily, I readily agreed and was stupid enough to keep the cigarettes in the very same pocket. About two weeks later, the scene repeated itself, but this time I didn't get off so easy. Daddy made me sit down in front of him while he watched me smoke a whole cigarette. In defiance and with false bravado, I did just that—the big twelve-year-old, smoking up a storm. I think his purpose was to embarrass me into quitting, and, although I never smoked in front of him, it did not diminish my desire to smoke. As I write this, forty-three years later, I am still battling with this addiction. This creates its own unique problems, because I am now a hypnotherapist who helps many people to become successful non-smokers. It is very true that one has to truly want to change before any real change can take place.

When I say that Connie and I drifted apart because of change, I mean that they changed drastically and painfully. All of the boys who had previously worked on the farm moved to Oshawa to take jobs at General Motors. Betty had finished high school and moved to Belleville to a full-time job. That left only Monie, Daddy, and me at home, and there was no way Daddy could continue to run the farm. For the first year of high school, I used to get up in the morning, go get the cows, and then milk my half of them before I got on the bus for school. As Monie had never had any interest in going near the barn, Daddy and I did all the milking and the day-to-day chores that were required for farm life.

Daddy finally had to make a decision to sell the family farm. As our land was divided by a road, he sold one parcel of two hundred acres to one brother whose land adjoined ours and eighty-nine acres to the other brother who adjoined us on the other side of the road. We kept the one acre of land that the little house sat on.

We had a big auction, and it was a sad day, with people from all over the area coming and buying up our stuff. The upside was that Daddy got $17,000 for the farm, which seemed like a lot of money. He got another couple of thousand from the auction and we all had a lot less work to do, so life seemed pretty easy for a while.

At some point during this time, Daddy was somehow convinced by his sister, Aunt Leona, to go with her to a singles' club called Club 39. She had been a widow for many years and I guess she thought that Daddy could use some companionship, so she set her sights on finding him a woman. He met a woman name Hilda, whom he took a liking to. I'm not sure how long he went out with her, but eventually he brought her home to meet all of us. It happened that he brought her home on a weekend when the whole family was home, and the family did not take kindly to her. I vaguely remember them teasing and tormenting her, and, when Daddy told us that he was considering marrying her, Helen very promptly announced, "I wasn't at your first wedding, and I sure as hell won't be at your second one." Poor Hilda got so upset that she left the house and starting walking back to Belleville, which was twenty-three miles away. Daddy went after her and drove her home. We never did see her again, and that was okay with us! I'm not sure about the whole story, but somehow it became known that when Hilda left the scene, most of Daddy's savings went with her.

Daddy eventually found someone else named Alice, whom he spent a lot of time with but he never brought her home. There was a period of time when he stayed away from home quite frequently, and, at those times, he was with her at a motel in Belleville. To this day, I don't remember if the relationship ended or if he was involved with her to the end. I may have blocked that period from my memory, because I don't want to think that someone else may have come before us kids in his priorities.

One of the times when he was away, Monie and I were at home alone because we were too young yet to be going out to dances or on dates. All the older kids had gone out for the night, and we heard a noise outside. Because in the past, even though we lived in the middle of nowhere, we had been subject to peeping toms and suspicious people coming around, Monie and I got scared and crept upstairs to hide. There were some boxes of clothes lined up under the eaves along one wall, and we crawled into them and made ourselves as small as we could. We were both scared, because we heard whoever it was come into the house.

At one point, Monie was crying because there were mice in there and one pooped on her. I told to her to hush, and we tried to huddle down even further. We could hear the person moving around, and we stayed as quiet as we could. Eventually, someone in the family came home, the police were called, and all of a sudden, there was a situation.

The person who had broken into our home was a man named Andy. He lived in a shack on the edge of Tweed, and everyone believed he was crazy. He was also a wino and had the strength of a bull. Not too many people wanted to tangle with him. The police came, and they tried to talk Andy into coming out of the house. He refused and told the police that he had dynamite and that he was going to blow up the house. I don't know if he knew Monie and I were in there or even cared if he did know. Things were quite tense for awhile but eventually they did get him out peacefully. The dynamite ended up being a plug of chewing tobacco that he had found in the house. In the time that he had been in there, he had drank shaving lotion that Daddy had gotten for Christmas, as well as stealing whatever he could and stashing it across the road. We found it later on when we went looking for the stuff that was missing. This was also the last time that Monie and I were left alone until we were older.

While we were living in the little house, I learned to drive a lot better. After the tractor, I learned to drive an old 1949 Dodge truck with a stick shift on the floor, and, by the time I was eleven years old, Daddy used to brag that I was a really good driver. He even let me drive our family car until the day that I pulled into the yard and ran into the house. Daddy wasn't home but everyone else was and took great pride in making fun of me, especially Carl, which really pissed me off because he wasn't usually mean. He was on the inside of the screen door teasing me and had the door locked so I couldn't come in.

I had a wicked temper. I got so mad at Carl for not letting me in that I kicked the new screen door in. Once I had done that, I panicked and off I ran. Carl and Tom, Helen's husband, weren't about to let me get away, and the chase was on. I ran through the cornfields and did my best to get away from them, but they had the dog with them. Eventually, they found me and dragged me back to the house. I was hot, exhausted, and totally furious. I climbed up the ladder to the upstairs and just laid on the floor in despair. Helen tells the story that she finally got me down by bribing me with a cold pop. Needless to say, Daddy was not very happy, and I don't think he bragged about my driving for a long time after that!

Chapter 10
Growing up Is Not Always Fun

On December first of my tenth grade year, I woke up one night and heard Daddy going up and down the ladder that led upstairs in the little house. This house was built by Ma and Daddy when they got married and was insulated with straw, as was common in that day and age. Because it was unusual for Daddy to go upstairs at all, I asked him what he was doing. He told me not to worry about it and to go back to sleep. Of course, there was no way, I could go back to sleep with this unusual activity going on, and I soon figured out that he was carrying buckets of water upstairs. I could also smell smoke, so I jumped out of bed and called the volunteer fire department that had been set up after our big house had burned. While we were waiting for them, we started carrying as much of our stuff as we could out of the house. We managed to get many of smaller items out but still lost a good deal of our belongings.

The fire in the woodstove had gotten too hot, and the straw insulation between the ceiling and the upstairs floor had caught on fire. Daddy, Monie, and I worked as hard as we could to salvage everything possible, and I was busy grabbing laundry soap and cleaning stuff off a shelf by the stove when the ceiling caved in. I was covered with black, smoky water from the fire hose. At this point, we were forced to watch helplessly as everything burned to the ground.

Once the firemen had done all they could, Monie and Daddy and I were taken up to Aunt Thelma and Uncle Bill's place. Uncle Bill was Daddy's only brother who lived close by, and he and his wife owned the general store in the tiny little village of Stoco. I don't think Aunt Thelma ever really approved of us, and I know I was a pretty sorry sight

41

when I walked through their door that morning. Not only was I black and wet from the smoke, I also smelled pretty bad. To her credit, Aunt Thelma immediately took us under her wing. Her home was always clean and organized, and she even kept supplies in her spare bedroom in case visitors needed anything. She had baby clothes and blankets, extra nightgowns and everything else that a visitor could possibly need.. I was impressed with this, and, to this day, I do the very same thing.

We stayed with Aunt Thelma and Uncle Bill for a few days and then found a house for rent just up the street from the store. By Christmas we were settled into the house in Stoco, and the few things that we had managed to salvage smelled like smoke for many more months. The only redeeming quality this time around was that we had insurance on the little house, so at least we had some extra funds to buy what we needed. There was even a little bit of extra money for Christmas, and Daddy bought me a brand-new winter coat and my first pair of figure skates, which I only recently let go of.

Once again, Daddy picked up the pieces of his life and did his best to provide for Monie and me. Then, at the end of January, less than two months after the little house burned, we were once again plagued with bad luck, which caused a dramatic change in the direction my life would take. On January 26, 1968, Monie and I came home from school. When we walked in the door, Daddy was laying in the middle of the living room floor in his underwear. He had gotten up in the morning to go to the bathroom, had suffered a major stroke, and fell onto the floor in the living room. He had been lying there all day, unable to move. To make it worse, the house we were living in was really a cottage with no basement and just a wall-mounted furnace. The floor was always freezing cold, and I'm sure that must have made things even worse for Daddy. I remember the date because it was the anniversary of Ma's death, and we were supposed to go to a Mass for her that evening.

I managed to get Daddy back into his bed and then called Aunt Thelma. She called the doctor, who told us to keep him in bed and, if he wasn't better by Monday, to bring him in to see him. For some reason that I can't remember, our older sisters and brothers didn't come home that weekend, and I did my best to take care of Daddy. No one really took this illness too seriously, and I'm not even sure anyone even knew it was a stroke. I sure as hell didn't know what a stroke was, and as a fairly mature, fourteen-year-old, all I knew was to feed him and try to keep him warm.

What did scare the hell out of me, was, that by Sunday night, when he looked at me, his eyes were kind of wild, and I wasn't even sure that he knew who I was. I called Aunt Thelma again and this time they came and took him to the hospital in Belleville. Within a few days, Belleville Hospital had transferred him to Kingston Hospital because they said he had a blood clot in his brain. I don't consciously remember anything being said about a stroke, but then again I was considered too young to be consulted much on what was going on with Daddy.

Daddy remained in Kingston Hospital until the beginning of April. We were able to go down and see him a few times on weekends when someone was available with a car. Monie and I were supposed to stay at Aunt Thelma's, but I think that we were so used to doing whatever we wanted that we balked at any attempt to conform to her rules. Consequently, Monie and I moved back to our own house and carried on the best we could. We managed to look after ourselves quite well. The grown-ups in the family still came home every weekend, so we weren't entirely left to our devices. Nevertheless, we managed to get ourselves into some situations that were not good.

One afternoon we skipped school. There were about six of us, and we went to this kid's house in downtown Tweed because his dad was at work. The guy whose house we were at was a little weird, but it was a place for us to sit around and hang out. We were feeling pretty good about getting out of school for the afternoon when this guy came into the room with one of his dad's guns. He refused to let any of us leave and scared the hell out of us by holding us hostages until it was time to catch the bus home. I don't remember a lot of details about that afternoon, but I do know that we stayed far away from him from then on. Of course, we couldn't say anything, because we weren't supposed to be there in the first place.

On Good Friday of the same year, Monie and I were in Tweed hanging out with our friends, and we stayed later than we should have. Our house was straight across the lake, and usually we walked home around the roads. Because we were late, I immediately reverted to one of my bright ideas. There was still ice on the lake, so I figured we could just walk straight across the lake and get home in less than half the time. Monie agreed, but with strong trepidation and we began our trek across the lake. When we were about halfway across, we realized the channel was open, and there was running water very close to where we were walking. I could not be deterred, and I sure as heck was not turning back so we kept going. We were both scared shitless and crept across the lake holding hands and saying prayers as we went. The ice was sinking under the water as we walked, and, to this day, I am still amazed that we made it home without drowning. Our guardian angels must have been with us on that trip. Needless to say, we never crossed that lake again, winter or summer!

During this growing up period, with all the freedom that we had, and living in such a small town, we were still influenced by the outside world. The Beatles were popular even in Stoco, and hippie culture had crept in. Some of my friends and I used to go to the golf course and experiment with "drugs"—not the popular drugs like marijuana or hash, but someone (not me) heard about the wonderful properties of sniffing glue and nail polish remover, so that's what we used. Talk about stupid! But we weren't aware of the consequences of our actions, and as I look back I think that we were all darn lucky that we made it through this phase. Again, there must have been guardian angels watching over us!

Our freedom provided a never-ending cause for adventure. I was never short of dates, and, from the time I was about twelve years old, I always had a boyfriend. During the time that Daddy was in the hospital, I met Bill, who was quite a bit older than I was. As a matter of fact, he was nine years older than I was, but keep in mind that I was a very mature fourteen. I could get into bars without ID from the time I was fourteen. Anyway, Bill and I started going steady after awhile. and he was a pillar that I could lean on. When I look back now, I wonder what was really going on, but at the time I was in the safest relationship that I would ever be in until I met my current husband. Bill never tried to force me into a sexual relationship, and the furthest that we ever went during the year and a half that I went out with him was necking. Of course, my family didn't know that, and they discouraged the relationship for a long time until they realized that I was not giving him up. Then they accepted that he was almost part of the family. As I said he was someone that I could lean on and depend on and during the next little while, I don't know what I would have done without him.

Chapter 11
Pain and Suffering Are Powerful Lessons

To our great relief, Daddy was released from the hospital and allowed to come home in early April. I think Monie and I were certainly looking forward to life getting back to normal again. The day that Daddy came home, the first thing he wanted to do was to walk around a bit outside. It was a beautiful spring day with sunshine that was beginning to warm up the earth, and I guess the farmer in him craved the smell of the land after that horrible hospital experience. While he was wandering slowly around the yard using his cane for the support he needed, I went across the road to get two pails of water from the neighbors' well because we still did not have indoor plumbing.

While I was gone, Daddy decided to smoke his pipe. While lighting it, I guess he was still pretty shaky, and he dropped the wooden match that he had been lighting his pipe with. As I came across the road with water, all I could see was Daddy on fire. The grass around him was on fire and so were his clothes. I ran as fast as I could, pushed him down, rolled him over, and then threw the two pails of water on him. With the fire out, I helped him into the car and rushed him to the doctor. His pants had been burned pretty much off, and his shoes had melted right into his skin. Needless to say, I was feeling sheer terror and drove to the doctor's at record speed. What came next still blows my mind to this day.

The doctor got his shoes off of him, peeling the skin from the bottom of his legs and feet right along with them. The doctor then sprayed him with something that was supposed to numb the pain and then sent him back home with me—a damned fourteen-year-old kid! And what the hell did I know? Doctor's were authority figures who supposedly knew what was best for their patients, so I did as I was told, took him back home with me, and made out the best I could.

The next day as I was walking over to get something in the kitchen, I saw Daddy sitting on a kitchen chair beside the phone. He was holding onto to his cane, and to this day I can still close my eyes and see the look of pain on his face and how purple his hands were because he had such a grip on that cane. He must have been in such incredible pain, and what I saw in his hands and in his eyes that day is still indescribable. I called Aunt Thelma, this time in tears, because the situation was so awful. She took matters into her own hands, and once again Daddy went into the hospital. The difference this time was that he was never coming home.

Daddy remained in Kingston Hospital until he died in July of that same year. We still managed to see him on weekends, but only for a few brief minutes because he was in intensive care. He was on one of those beds where they would put a board over top of him and flip him occasionally. The doctors attempted skin grafts, but I think that Daddy had given up on life. He suffered more strokes and seemed to be in constant pain. The last time that I saw him for a few minutes, the only thing he said was, "John, this is a son of bitching place!"

Not long after that, the hospital called us and told us to get his suit ready for his funeral. There was a lot of speculation and denial amongst the family as to whether there was a chance that Daddy would get well, but we couldn't dodge the inevitable. I know that I was in total denial. I figured that if his suit wasn't ready, he wouldn't die. I quickly learned that death comes whether we are ready or not. The thought of Daddy never coming back again was one of the harshest realities that I have ever had to face. He was waked at the Catholic funeral home in Tweed, and we had three days to watch over him and let reality set in. This was the first time that Betty and I were really and truly close. I remember us hugging each other and sharing some of our feelings of loss together.

Our brother Reg was in Algonquin Park camping when Daddy died, and we had to get the OPP to find him and tell him. He arrived the day of the funeral, and it was a horrible time for him because he and Daddy had had an argument some time back and had not spoken since. I remember Reg being inconsolable, and I've often thought that this must have been a terrible burden of guilt for him to bear.

After the funeral, there was a gathering of the family and some friends at our house. It seemed as though we had just gotten back to the house when an argument between my sister Helen and my second-oldest brother Joe started. The heated discussion quickly spread throughout the group, and I was in disbelief that this could be happening. I ran away. I didn't go far, just to a neighbor's house, but I refused to go back home again. All I wanted was for Daddy to come back home and everything to be the way it used to be.

Once the funeral was over and things started to settle down, there was some discussion around what to do with Monie and me. Originally, it was decided that Betty and Lois, who both worked in Belleville, would move back home with us until we finished high school. Mona was going into grade ten, and I was going into grade eleven. After my refusal to come back home, they looked at other options, and Helen had enough room for one. So she agreed to take Mona to Oshawa to live with her until she finished her schooling.

Reg's wife, Brenda, came down to see me and asked if I would consider living with them in Oshawa to finish school. I gave it a lot of thought, but really I don't think I had much choice in the matter. At any rate, the idea did appeal to me, and the next thing I knew, we were packing our personal stuff and moving to Oshawa. I had been to Oshawa once before and thought it was a big city with its 51,000 people. It was a General Motors town, and, after their hiring blitz in the mid-1960s, almost everyone we knew worked there. It was big money with great benefits for many people from small towns like Tweed.

My family decided to keep the house that we were renting in Stoco so that we could all come home on weekends. I think that they divvied up the forty dollar a month rent, and most of us continued to come home from Oshawa and Belleville every weekend. Most of the time, I traveled back and forth with Bill because he worked at Goodyear Tire, which was in Bowmanville, just a stone's throw away from Oshawa. We would go home to Stoco, and, every Sunday night before heading back to Oshawa, we would go to his mom's for Sunday dinner. They had finally accepted that I might one day be part of their family, and Bill's dad even made me a hope chest out of cedar that we had begun to fill with necessities. At that time, Texaco Gas was giving away glasses and dishes, and we made a point out of adding them to the hope chest whenever we could.

On one of these trips back to Oshawa, we gave an uncle of Bill's a ride to Oshawa and dropped him off at the Queen's Hotel, where he was meeting up with some friends. A few years later, I learned that the friends he was meeting were the grandparents of the man that I actually married! Talk about a small world!

Chapter 12
It's a Working World

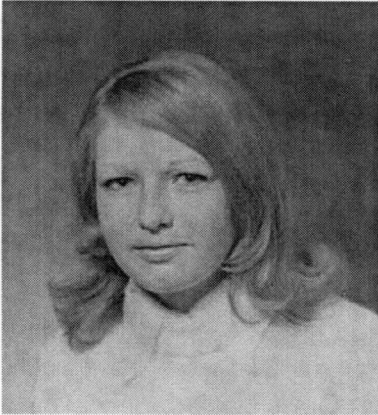

My move to Oshawa began some significant changes in my life, mainly in realizing that if I wanted to go anywhere with my life, it was going to be up to me. I attended school every day and started to pay attention. I became introverted and decided that I would remain anonymous, minding my own business and finishing my education.

When I moved in with Reg and Brenda, it was agreed that I would receive my "baby bonus" money every month, which amounted to about twelve dollars. As I was already a smoker and required clothing and so forth for school, I decided that I needed a part-time job. I got the first job that I applied for, which was as a carhop at the local A&W. I came home excited about what I considered to be my first professional job. I had always worked to make money, but so far it had just been unimportant things like babysitting and sweeping and cleaning the local barbershop in Tweed, but this was the real deal. I was going to be paying income tax and receiving a proper paycheck! When I got home and told Reg about my new job, he asked me how I got the job when I was only fifteen years old. I admitted that I had lied about my age. After giving me a lecture about being honest, he immediately drove me back to the A&W and made me tell the manager that I wasn't sixteen. Thank goodness, the manager overlooked that fact and allowed me to start the job anyway. It involved many late hours because they stayed open late, but that was okay with me. I worked every opportunity that I could.

Working as a carhop at the A&W opened my eyes to another aspect of this wonderful world. I no longer had many of the previous responsibilities that I had had before. I didn't have to come home from school and make meals, do dishes, or clean house. I helped out, of course, but it was no longer my responsibility. I became a somewhat normal fifteen-year-old. Interest in boys my own age started to emerge, and it was a tough time for me and Bill. I began seeing what I was missing out on and decided to break it off with him. It was not an easy thing to do, and we both took the breakup quite badly. Up until this point Bill, I, and both of our families had assumed that Bill and I would eventually get married. I think that both families were somewhat relieved when we broke up because of the age difference. So we parted but still remained a part of each other's lives for a while. I continued to work as much as I could, meeting a lot of people my own age. I found my niche at school with three of my classmates, and before long I began dating again.

I dated quite a few guys but never more than a few months at a time and never very seriously. I had made a decision to join the armed forces when I finished school, and I was determined that nothing would stand in my way. This would give me time to make a decision about what I wanted to do with my life, while at the same time seeing more of the world and furthering my education, which I could not afford to do on my own. It's amazing how fate intervenes and blows away your plans as if they were nothing more than fluff in the wind.

When I first started working at the A&W, there was a sign on the wall that read: "If a 1963 Pontiac convertible, white with a black top, comes onto the parking lot, please inform the manager." It didn't take me long to figure out who they were talking about. It was a guy who everyone knew only as Moose. His best friend Richard had an identical car, except Moose's had a red interior with red sex lights and Richard's had a blue interior with blue sex lights. They would come into the A&W every day. One of their favorite things to do was to park a car on each side of the building and rev their engines. They had really noisy mufflers, and, when they did this, if you were inside the building, you couldn't hear a thing. It made it difficult to hear or to take orders, so the manager would get annoyed and call the police. One time I heard him complaining to the police, and they replied, "Oh hell, it's only Moose," which frustrated the manager even more. (As I write about this event some thirty-seven years later, this same manager has hired Moose, who is now my husband, to landscape his house.)

It seemed that every time Moose came onto the lot, he was with a different girl. He was obviously very popular, and it seemed as if everyone knew him. If there was a fight anywhere, it was a sure bet that he was involved in it. Sometimes guys would start a fight and then depend on Moose to get them out of it without them getting hurt too much. His friend Richard was never far from his side, and many times looked out for Moose when he had too much to drink. I even saw Richard making sure Moose's date got home safely when Moose wasn't able to do so. Moose even asked *me* out a couple of times. But he was way too wild for me, and I wasn't about to go there. Going out with him would get me into situations that I wasn't ready for. He was not the type of guy that you could go out with and get by with just a goodnight kiss. I just acted like I thought he was fooling around with me and never said yes.

One New Year's Eve, the manager of the A&W decided that they would stay open late and asked for volunteers to work that night. As I had just broken up with the guy I was going out with and had no special plans for the evening, I volunteered to work. Another girl, Jackie, and I decided that if we were going to work, we might as well celebrate while we worked. We pooled our money and bought a mickey bottle of booze and brought it into work. We spiked our Cokes in the staff room and kept going back throughout our shift for a drink. Considering that neither of us were drinkers, it didn't take much to get us pretty happy, but we still managed to do our job without any problems.

I was feeling pretty good, and, just before midnight, Moose rolled in and ordered his usual: Whistle Dog and Coke. When I delivered it to him, I was feeling quite daring, and he was flirting like crazy with me. Somehow, he talked me into leaving my wristwatch with him so that he would know when it was midnight. In order to get it back, I would have to give him a New Year's kiss to celebrate. Feeling a lot less inhibited, I agreed and then, after I gave him a quick kiss at midnight,

51

he refused to give me my watch back until I went out on a date with him. I made some excuse and got away. I figured my watch was long gone because I would not be going out with him!

By the time I had finished my shift, I was very drunk and just wanted to go home. This guy, Darryl, whom I had gone out with months before, was hanging around, and he offered to give me a ride home. He got a little nasty when I did not allow him to come into the house with me, and thank goodness I didn't tell him that I was home alone for the holiday. I was able to get rid of him, and, once I got inside the door of my house, I barely made it upstairs before I was violently sick. As I had never been drunk before, it was a very unpleasant experience, and afterward I began feeling very sorry for myself.

Around six in the morning I had the worst headache I had ever had in my life, and I think it scared me. I called Jim, the guy who I had just broken up with a few weeks before. Jim took his brother's car and came right over. He held my hand and nursed me through the worst of it, and it wasn't too long before there was another knock on the door.

To our surprise, there on the doorstep was Jim's dad, and, boy, was he mad. Jim made up a quick story about me being all alone for New Year's and that I was depressed because of all that I had been through. Then he told his dad that I had tried to commit suicide, and that's why he had taken his brother's car and rushed over. Jim's dad immediately changed from being angry to being concerned and told Jim to bring me to their house for New Year's dinner when I felt like getting up. We had no choice but to carry on with the charade, or else Jim would have been in serious trouble, so I went to their house for dinner. They lived in an upscale neighborhood called Beau Valley, and their house was the fanciest thing that I have ever seen. I was out of my comfort zone, but that family did everything they could to make me feel comfortable. Talk about being a fraud! They were obviously wonderful, caring, and supportive parents, and Jim was following in their footprints. Jim and I didn't get back together and I haven't seen him for over forty years, but I still have great feelings of respect for him and what he did for me that day.

Things simmered down after that, and I never really went out with anyone else for about six weeks. Moose kept asking me out, and, erring on the side of safety, I finally agreed that my best friend Louise and I would go for a ride with him and his friend Brian one evening.

When that evening came, Louise and I did an incredibly stupid thing. At school we hung around with a rather strange crowd of misfits. One of the guys in this group, Peter, could acquire anything you needed, including illegal substances. He used to offer us different things, and one night Louise and I decided to take him up on his offer to try some marijuana. We went to an abandoned building at the local airport and smoked up. By the time that we got back home, it was almost time for Moose and Brian to pick us up. We were really stoned, and Louise had the giggles the whole time. I was feeling incredibly frustrated because I couldn't think straight. Louise and I both stayed in the backseat and refused to pair off, and thankfully the boys took us home fairly quickly. I guess the good thing that came out of this experience was that I decided drugs were not for me, because I preferred to be in full control of my mind.

Moose continued to ask me out, and I kept putting him off until one Saturday afternoon when he came into the A&W. He was on a lunch break from his job as an apprentice mechanic at a local car dealership, and this time he got out of his car and came right into the building to order his food. When he started flirting with me, I noticed that he had the most engaging smile, and, for the first time since I had known him, he was sober. He seemed so different this way, and, when he asked me out on the pretense of returning my watch, I agreed, as long as he would tell me his real name and was not drinking. He told me his name was Bruce, and we agreed to go out on the following Friday night to a dance at the Jube, which was the hot spot to go in those days.

True to his word, when he picked me up on Friday night, he was sober and did not have a drink all night. As he had picked me up early, we went to the A&W for a Coke before going to the dance. We started talking, and, before we knew it, a few hours had gone by. We went to the dance for a while and then left. This time we went to another drive-in restaurant for something to eat and a Coke and once again started talking. Before we knew it, it was almost three o'clock in the morning. He took me home and settled for a mere kiss goodnight! It was February 13, 1970.

The next night when I got off work, he was waiting for me. This time he wasn't driving his own car. He was stone-cold sober and with a friend who was an off-duty police officer. We double-dated with this other couple, and, before the night was out, he asked me to go steady. I have to say that in my innocence, I believed that he had changed almost literally overnight, and I agreed to be his only girlfriend.

It is hard to believe that it has taken me over a year to get this far; however, the memories remain strong and clear, and Louie, my inner voice, and I continue to feel an ever-increasing need to complete it. (May 20, 2006)

Chapter 13
Is This Love?

Having Bruce in my life changed everything. It seemed that every minute that I wasn't working or in school was spent with him. Having all this attention from someone so popular and well liked was a disconcerting experience. Our days were spent driving around the countryside and having long talks about everything. Until I had gone out with him, whenever I asked anyone what his story was, no one seemed to know much. It was like, all of a sudden, someone was truly interested in who he was, and he had completely opened up. As we became more comfortable together, he began to share everything about his life, including the good, the bad, and the ugly from his past.

I cannot tell you all of it here because that is his story to tell, and a very inspiring one it is. I keep telling him that he should write his own book! I can tell you that both of his parents were deaf and mute, and that he, his brother, and his mom lived with his grandmother. Bruce had gotten into some trouble in his youth and had spent time in foster homes and youth correctional facilities until he was about fifteen. After all he had been through, he had made the choice to straighten his life out, even if all of the adults in his life did not truly believe that he could. Straightening himself out did not mean that he became an angel, by any means. When I started going out with him, he had a giant chip on his shoulder and was a true "bad boy." I naïvely thought that I had fixed him!

As we moved forward with our relationship, things began to change. Bruce would show up late for dates smelling of booze and would always have an excuse. One time that stands out—and that we joke about now—was when he called me and told me that he had knocked himself out in the bathtub, had just come to, and would be over to pick me up shortly. His drinking became a major issue in our relationship, and then something happened that forced me into the decision to break up with him.

Bruce wanted total commitment, and he wanted to be together every spare minute. Even when I told him that I wanted to stay in to spend the evening washing my hair and catching up on personal chores, he would call every half hour. One time, he even sat in the churchyard across the street from my house to make sure I wasn't going out with someone else. It got so bad that, at one point, my girlfriend Louise and I took the bus to my sister Helen's house right after school to avoid him. I told Brenda that when he called to tell him that she didn't know where I was. Later on, she called me at Helen's and told me that he was driving her crazy, calling and calling, so I relented and told her to have him call me at Helen's house. He called and wanted to come and get me, so, seeing as it was getting late and I had to get home, I told him that he could come and give us a ride home. When he showed up, he was pretty inebriated, and the ride home was the ride from hell. Louise and I clung to each other in fear and prayed that we would make it home in one piece. I didn't say much until after we had dropped Louise off, and, by the time we reached my driveway, I was furious. I told Bruce that I had had enough and couldn't handle his possessiveness and drinking any more. Naturally, he was very upset and threatened to do himself harm if I carried through with the breakup. With false bravado, I told him that I didn't care and let him go. However, I sat up all night listening to the local radio station and worrying myself sick about him. I was greatly relieved when he pulled up to the school the next day, but it did not lessen my resolve to stay away from him.

Bruce did not give up easily and continued to call me and to show up at school. I had no choice but to see him when I was working because the A&W was his place to hang out. I stayed true to my convictions for a while and even started to see Bill again, even though I knew that the relationship with him could not be revived.

A few weeks after my breakup with Bruce, he called me at the house in Stoco and just wanted to talk. He asked if he quit drinking would I reconsider. I told him that I would, and the next day there he was at our little house in Stoco to see me. We did an awful lot of talking, and I agreed to get back together with him if he agreed to quit drinking. He shared an incident that had happened the week before that was to have a major impact on our lives. As I relate this incident, keep in mind that drinking and driving in those days was not regarded as the extremely serious crime that it is considered today. Although it was frowned upon, it was given much less importance and punishment by the courts.

Bruce drove a 1963 Pontiac that was in pretty good shape, considering that he was apprenticing to be a mechanic; however, the key didn't work for the trunk and he had to use a screwdriver to open it. One of the things that he was known for was having a trunk full of beer and a bottle of rye on hand. Everyone knew where the screwdriver was kept, including quite a few of the local cops, whom Bruce knew well in those days. Most of the time, when Bruce was not in the greatest shape to drive, they would make sure that he made it home safe.

However, on one of these occasions when Bruce had had too much to drink, which just happened to be during the time that we were broken up, one of the cops, who was not one of his friends, decided to pull him over. Bruce made a break from him and raced home before the cop could catch him. Bruce's downfall was a signal light that did not turn off after he had turned the corner. Consequently, when he pulled into his driveway and got out of his car, his right signal light was still flashing, and the cop found him. Bruce was charged with drinking and driving, and this was the story that he had to tell me when he came down to see me that Sunday. I think that the charge scared him, and he was beginning to realize that this was not what he wanted out of his life.

We got back together, and Bruce promised to give up the booze, which he did for the most part. There were a few incidents after that, but they became fewer and fewer. Even so, my family still thought that my relationship with Bruce was a cause for concern. Bruce went to court about his drinking and driving charge and received a $200 fine or two weeks in jail. Since he didn't have the $200 and did not want to borrow it from his grandmother, he agreed to the two weeks in jail. He figured that he could take his holidays, serve his time, and save himself some money. If only it were that easy!

He was to report to the police station to be taken into custody to serve his sentence on a specified date. I dropped him off, and a few hours later he called me to come get him. It seems they didn't have room for him at the Whitby Jail. This happened two more times before they finally admitted him into the jail. Whitby Jail was only about fifteen minutes away from where we lived, so it seemed easy enough to be able to go visit, and, after all, it was only for two weeks.

He was finally admitted into the jail on a Thursday. What Bruce didn't know was that on Fridays the jail was cleared in anticipation of people they would be picking up over the weekend. When they came to tell Bruce that they were moving him up to the Don Jail in Toronto, Bruce told them that he wasn't going anywhere. Well, we all know who usually wins in these situations, and Bruce learned the hard way. He was taken to the Don Jail and placed into solitary confinement for hitting the guard. He was there for a few days and remained belligerent when they finally let him out of the hole. After yet another altercation, he was further confined and shipped off to Mimico Correctional Facility in another part of Toronto to finish out his sentence. When he eventually agreed to behave himself, he was placed into the general population and finally allowed a phone call. He called me and told me to go see his grandmother and borrow the $90 that it would take to pay the balance due on his fine and to get him to hell out of there.

I went to see his grandmother, and she reluctantly gave me the money to bail him out. Bruce had given me his car to drive while he was away. Driving around Oshawa was one thing in those days, but for me, a sixteen-year-old and a fairly new licensed driver, to drive into Toronto was a whole other story. I didn't even know where Mimico was; I just knew it was somewhere in Toronto. I asked Bruce's brother Glen to come with me to pick him up, and on a hot, sunny summer's day in July, we headed out. Bruce drove a 1963 Pontiac convertible, so it was only fitting to drive with the top down. I was glad that we made that decision, because hours later, when we finally found him, he was wearing an orange prison jumpsuit and was sweating his ass off cutting the grass on the prison grounds. We paid his fine, had him released, and set off for home. Bruce had not been able to have a shower for the nine days that he had been incarcerated, so you can imagine how he smelled. Boy, were we grateful to have the top down. When we got back to Oshawa, he had three showers before he managed to finally eradicate the smell of the prison!

A rather interesting little tidbit about Bruce's jail stint is the fact that he now runs a successful business in lawn maintenance and landscaping. I often joke that he got his career start in prison, but he's not as amused by it as I am.

Chapter 14
Moving Again

Around the same time that I was establishing a meaningful relationship with Bruce, another notable incident occurred that changed things for both of us. When I first moved to Oshawa, I lived with Reg and Brenda. All went well for a while, and then things slowly began to change. I don't know if my living with them created stress in their marriage, or if their marriage would have suffered even if I had not been there. I was in school during the day and working as much as I could in the evening, so I really wasn't there a whole lot. Even so, Brenda seemed to turn against me. A lot of the things that she did didn't make a lot of sense to me. If I was out at night and my curfew was ten o'clock, I would always make sure that I was in the driveway well ahead of my scheduled time. If I was in the driveway at twenty to ten, she would flash the outside lights until I came into the house. She would do this throughout the week, giving me the distinct impression that she didn't trust me. Then every Friday, she and Reg would pack up and go home for the weekend, leaving me alone and totally unsupervised for the whole weekend. Now wouldn't you think I would be more apt to get into trouble on the weekend when there was no one around to watch me?

As things continued to get worse, I tried to stay out of her way as much as possible. One Sunday before my graduation, I told her that Bruce was driving me down to Belleville to see Lois so that I could borrow a dress for my high school graduation ball. I certainly couldn't afford to buy one, and, as Lois had quite a few dresses that she had worn as a bridesmaid, she generously offered to loan me one. Bruce and I spent most of the day with Lois, and I came home excited about the upcoming dance when I would get to dress up and look beautiful.

When I got home from Belleville around ten o'clock that night, Reg was waiting up for me. He was furious because he had no idea where I had been. We had a big fight, and I told him that Brenda knew where I was and was supposed to have told him. Obviously, this did not help my situation with Brenda, and I made the decision that it was time to leave. The next day, Bruce drove me over to their place to pick up my belongings, and, when I tried to go upstairs to get my clothes, Brenda met me at the top of the steps and we had a physical altercation, with her trying to push me down the steps. It's a good thing that she didn't succeed, because she had the wringer washer going and it was parked right at the bottom of the steps. She didn't succeed because Bruce stepped in to break things up. I got my stuff and went to stay at Helen's house, which was a temporary solution because Helen and Tom already had three children and were living in a two-bedroom apartment. Monie was staying with them as well, but, because she was down in Belleville babysitting for the summer, there was a short-term bed for me to sleep in. Before Monie came back, I had found a room in a rooming house where I could afford the rent of twelve dollars a week.

The rooming house that I moved into was in a nice, respectable neighborhood, and the landlady was renting rooms because her husband had left her and she needed the extra income so that she wouldn't lose her home. I got along well with the other tenants, and we had full run of the entire house. After I had been there for a while, I realized that my landlady had a problem with taking all kinds of pills and downing them with brandy and milk. A number of times, she was taken to the hospital by whoever found her passed out. Sometimes that was Bruce and me, and most of us felt responsible for her because her own family no longer wanted anything to do with her. I lived in this house until I got married the following November, but I am getting ahead of myself again.

After Bruce's stint in jail and my moving out on my own, we both grew up a lot. We both realized that we only had ourselves and each other to rely on, and that life was a major responsibility. Bruce was still working as an apprentice mechanic at a local GM dealership, and I continued to work part time at the A&W. As I was almost finished with high school, it was time to get a full-time job. Around the same time, Bruce was laid off from his job, so both of us required employment.

One day we found two ads in the local paper for the Canadian Tire Store. I applied for the office job, and Bruce applied for parts counter. Lo and behold, we both got hired on the same day. During our interviews, we were told that as employees there was no dating of other employees allowed, so we never let on that we knew each other. I also kept my job at the A&W on weekends to bring in extra income. We were sitting in the car one night in mid-September, debating on getting another car, because the one that Bruce had was getting pretty rough. Out of the blue, he asked me how soon we could get married. It was either a new car or a marriage, and we opted for November 21, 1970 as our wedding date. I was seventeen, and Bruce was nineteen. Both of us thought we were pretty grown up!

A few weeks later, when Bruce came in for his usual Whistle Dog and root beer, I went to pick his tray up, and there on the tray was a set of wedding bands. Bruce had gone shopping at K-mart and couldn't resist picking them up. They must have been a pretty good deal, because thirty-eight years later we both still proudly wear them. We certainly couldn't afford a diamond engagement ring, so that would have to wait. (I did get one thirteen years later.)

As we got busy planning our wedding, which was only two months away, we tried to stay within our meager financial means. I borrowed Helen's wedding dress, and our landlady offered us the use of her house for our reception. We borrowed $2000 from the credit union and used it to put two month's rent down on a basement apartment. We were also able to buy a three-room grouping of furniture, which was very popular in those days. The rest of the money was spent on wedding preparations. But even during this time, there were events that kept things from going too smoothly.

The rooming house where I was staying had a vacant room, and the landlady had placed an ad in the local paper. Only one person applied for it, and the night that he came to see the room, the landlady was in one of her inebriated states. I talked to Ron, the perspective tenant, and, although he was older and dressed in outdated clothing, he was polite and seemed okay. He paid the rent up front and moved in. From the moment he moved in, he set out to become indispensable to the landlady and the other tenants, particularly one of the young girls who was also living there. In a few short weeks, he had won everyone's trust and almost seemed to rule the house. He was always polite and fatherly with me, and, like the others, I trusted him. He always had a solution to our problems and gave the right advice when we needed it. He somehow got involved in our wedding plans and had us believing that he was fairly well-to-do financially. He even gave us an envelope with our name on it that was not to be opened until our wedding day. He told us that it was his wedding gift to us and that it was airline tickets and a booking for a hotel room for our honeymoon. We believed him and did not open the envelope.

One of the problems that he had a solution for had to do with our furniture purchase. When our new furniture was delivered, the chesterfield would not fit down the stairs to our little basement apartment. The furniture store agreed to rebate the cost of the chesterfield and would issue us a check the following week. In the meantime, we found a secondhand leather chesterfield for sale in the want ads. Ron suggested that he come with us to look at it, and, when we got there, the people wanted it gone as soon as possible because they were moving the next day. As we were not going to have the money for almost a week, Ron told us that he would write a check and that we could pay him back when we got our money. We agreed, paid for sofa with his check, and left with the furniture. We didn't think anything more about this until it was time for us to pick up the check at the furniture store the following week.

Bruce was working, and I was to pick up the check, meet Bruce on his break so that he could sign it, cash the check, and then meet Ron to give him the money that we owed him. When I met Bruce on his break, he was frantic. He had gotten a call from my landlady, who was also in a panic. Ron had borrowed her car and some money, and, for some eerie reason, she had felt a need to go into his room. When she did, all of his things were gone. She realized that all of the money that she had in the house as well as her jewelry was gone. The other young girl that was living in the house had moved all her things out as well.

We went with our landlady to the police station to make an incident report, but apparently Ron and the girl were long gone. We later found out that he had passed a number of bad checks; fortunately, we had not given him any of our hard-earned money! We spent a long time at the police station looking through mug shots but did not find him. The police told us that because of the way he had been dressed, he had probably just gotten out of jail and that we had been conned. Without being able to identify him, there was nothing more that we could do. When we went home and opened up the envelope that he had given us, it held nothing more than some newspaper clippings and blank pieces of paper. It was a strong lesson in trust for both Bruce and me and the beginning of our realization not to be ruled by greed. We were easily taken in by someone promising us something that in hindsight was unrealistic. We were lucky that we came through it financially unscathed, which could not be said for some of the others. Our landlady's car and the young girl were found a few days later at a motel in Scarborough, which is about a half hour away from Oshawa.

The night after the unveiling of the con artist, I didn't want to stay at the rooming house, so Monie agreed to stay with me at our apartment, which we had set up. Bruce was with us for a while, and then he left to go home. Monie and I got ready for bed, and, as soon as all the lights were out, my mind started going in all directions, worrying about this guy who had violated our trust. Every time I closed my eyes, Ron's face was all I could see. If I opened my eyes, I could swear that he was peaking in the windows. I fell into an uneasy sleep, and, sure enough, I dreamed about him. I woke up scared, went to the phone in the living room, and called Bruce's grandmother's house. She was sympathetic and told me that she would send Bruce down with a sleeping pill. At this point Monie was still sleeping, but my talking on the phone may have woken her up. As I passed through the kitchen on my way back to the bedroom, I reached into the drawer and pulled out the largest butcher knife I could find.

Poor Monie, not knowing what I had been going through in my mind, only saw this seemingly crazy person coming into the bedroom wielding a knife. I wasn't in any condition mentally to notice the look on her face, but, in retrospect, I'll bet it was it was a sight to behold! She asked me what I was doing, and I told her that I was waiting for Bruce. God knows what she was thinking then! Anyway, Bruce arrived with the promised sleeping pill, and I made him sleep on top of the covers in the middle of the bed to protect us.

Fortunately, we managed to put all of this behind us and carry on with the wedding. As I was only seventeen, I needed my guardian to sign for me to get married. Helen did this without asking any questions. I thought that was pretty cool until later on, when I found out that she signed the papers because she thought I was pregnant. In those days, if you were pregnant, you got married. I also found out much later that the family had some concerns that Bruce was not going to be good for me. They thought I would probably end up as a single mom on welfare and that he would be long gone. Bruce and I still joke that if we split up even now, thirty-eight years later, someone would probably say that they knew it wasn't going to last!

On the night before our wedding, we had the rehearsal, and Bruce's grandmother threw us a party afterward. I have to admit that she was pretty good about it, considering that, when we told her that we were getting married, all she said was, "You made your bed, and now you can lie in it." She was very often quite a demanding woman, and many, many of our dates were interrupted so that Bruce could pick her up from bingo and give her a ride home. I don't think he ever refused her request. Sometimes, one of the other five grandsons would do it, but the majority of the time it was Bruce. He was always good to her, and I think, in a way, he was always seeking her approval.

We attended our rehearsal at Kedron United Church, and I was pretty nervous, although I did not think I would be. During the rehearsal, I couldn't say my vows for the life of me, because I was too busy giggling. Everything seemed to be incredibly funny that night, and, at one point, Bruce was so upset at my attitude that he said he wouldn't marry me if I was the last person on Earth. Even that didn't deter the giddiness, and obviously he didn't mean it because he showed up for the wedding.

November 21, 1970, dawned as a beautiful, sunny, late fall day. My wedding party and I were up early to get our hair done before the eleven o'clock ceremony. On this day, I was as sober and serious as I had been giddy the night before. I was so calm and matter of fact that all the tittering and nervousness of the girls in my wedding party was driving me crazy, so I left them on their own to get ready, and I went downstairs to carve the turkey and the ham and to make sure all of the food was ready for the reception.

My brother Carl was giving me away, and we were alone for the ride to the church. As we were heading in that direction, Carl said, "Just say the word, John, and I'll head down home if you don't want to do this." I told him that this was what I wanted, so to the church we went. Within the hour, I was declared "Mrs. Dorothy Gagnon."

On the morning of our wedding, we did not even have enough money to leave town. We figured that we would probably spend our wedding night at our new apartment, but with the $60 that we received as part of our wedding gifts, we were able to head down the highway on a honeymoon.

We arrived in Kingston, about two hours away from Oshawa, at about nine o'clock at night and checked into the 401 Inn. We went downstairs and had a nice dinner and then went up to our room. We really thought that we were in high society when we realized that the bed had a vibrating unit in it. Bruce put his quarter in for the fifteen-minute thrill, and, when we woke up at five o'clock the next morning; we realized that the vibrating was still going on. I guess it had malfunctioned, so we really got our money's worth on that one.

We had a late breakfast and then made our way to Kingston Psychiatric Hospital, where Bruce's dad lived. He had lived there since Bruce was four years old, and that's a whole other story in itself. And, as I mentioned earlier, it is Bruce's story. Anyway, I met Bruce's dad for the first time, and then we headed back to Belleville for a visit with my brother Joe and his wife, Doreen, who had not been able to make it to the wedding. We had enough money left for another night in a hotel, so when we got to Belleville, we checked into the Ramada Inn before going to visit with Joe. When we arrived at Joe's house, he would not hear of us staying in a hotel room when they had a perfectly good single bed that we could sleep in. Joe knew the people who ran the hotel, and he got our money back. So Bruce and I spent the second night of our honeymoon cozied up in my nephew's single bed and afraid to do anything more than sleep because we might be heard by Joe and Doreen.

By Sunday night, we were back at home. To our surprise, we found things in quite a disarray in our apartment. Our family and friends had let themselves in to have some fun on our behalf. They did things like putting saran wrap over the toilet and strategically arranging Bruce's underwear in the middle of the bed with a cucumber in them! It was late and we were tired, but we finally managed to get everything cleaned up and to get settled into our first home. Neither of us could afford time off work, so both of us went back to work on Monday. One of us had to leave our job at Canadian Tire, and, because Bruce's job in the parts department paid more, I returned to my part-time job at the A&W until I could find full-time employment somewhere else.

It just happened that GM, who is a major employer in our area, was hiring. Bruce was fortunate to get hired on within a month after we were married. We felt that we had hit the big time when he landed that job! It paid more than twice what he was getting at Canadian Tire and had a pension and full benefits plan to boot. Talk about excited. It was like our dreams were beginning to come true.

Chapter 15
And Baby Makes Three

We settled down into domesticity, and then it was our first Christmas together. Bruce was working Christmas Eve, and I was over at Helen's, who with three kids was busy getting ready for Santa Claus's visit. She had some last-minute shopping to get finished, so I volunteered to drive her to the mall. Monie stayed to babysit her kids. Helen and I left to go shopping, and I completely forgot that my prescription for the pill was being delivered. I also forgot to leave Monie the money, and, when the guy came with my prescription, she didn't even have the thirty-five cents to pay for it. The delivery person from the pharmacy left with the prescription, and, by the time Helen and I arrived home, the stores were closed and it was too late to pick it up. Consequently, sometime over the Christmas season I became pregnant.

Because I was pregnant, I didn't think it was fair to get a full-time job and then have to leave after a few months. In those days, there was no such thing as maternity leave. You left your job six weeks before you were due and only got your job back if it was still available when you were ready to return. Also, at that time, most mothers stayed at home after they had children. Because of the circumstances, I continued working at the A&W and getting as many hours as I could until I didn't fit into my uniform anymore. Our thinking at this time was that with Bruce making such good money at GM we didn't have anything to worry about financially. How innocent we were!

Our baby was due at the end of September, and, during those years, GM would close for the summer and return to full production in September. Because we needed extra money, Bruce put his name in for summer work and was accepted into the parts department from

June until September. He worked most of the summer, and then, one Friday night near the end of his shift, he climbed a ladder to the higher bins to find some parts for an order. The ladder broke away from the wall, and Bruce plummeted to the floor from about twenty feet up. He landed on another guy who was picking parts from one of the lower bins and broke the other guy's shoulder.

They both ended up at the hospital; the other guy with his broken shoulder and Bruce with no apparent injuries at all. He was grinning all the way home at having tempted fate and come away the winner. It was a short-lived victory, because the next morning when he got out of bed, he was feeling a great deal of pain and he could not straighten up at all. For the next few days, he walked around with his nose about a foot from his knees. He had damaged his back and had very little mobility. On Monday, when Bruce went to the doctor, he was immediately sent to a specialist. Thus began a yearlong round of hospitals, physiotherapy, Workmen's Compensation, financial instability, and frustration. He was in and out of the hospital and fortunately was out when our son, Bradley Alexander, was born on October 12, 1971.

I know that I stated earlier that our baby was due in late September, but he was certainly in no rush to see the world. From mid-September until he was born on our Canadian Thanksgiving day in almost mid-October, I was at the doctor's office on a weekly basis. He kept telling me that I could go into labor at any time. It had been a fairly uneventful pregnancy, and it got to the point where I just wanted to get it over with. I wasn't the only one.

Bruce and his grandmother kept coming up with all kinds of ideas on how to speed up the baby's birth. Bruce would take me for rides over the roughest roads he could find, and his grandmother wanted me to take a dose of castor oil. There was no way I was going to take that yucky stuff, no matter how much I wanted the baby to be born. Bruce even encouraged me to jump down the last few steps to our basement apartment in hopes that it would work!

Finally, the doctor figured it was time to do something. He told me that I could go through Thanksgiving weekend and then on Tuesday, if the baby had not been born, they would put me in the hospital and induce labor. We were at Bruce's grandmother's for Thanksgiving dinner, and after the meal we spent the evening playing cards. It was one of those nights where every hand I was dealt was a winner. We were playing euchre, and I was getting loner hands and beating the pants off whomever I was playing against. Bruce's grandmother was not a graceful loser and kept joking that she would put me in the hospital herself if I kept on winning.

We finally went home to our little basement apartment and got into bed. About an hour and a half after we were in bed, I felt a pop, and Bruce, thinking I was being rude and passing gas, turned his back to me. I felt a whoosh and realized that my water had broken. I jumped out of bed, telling Bruce that it wasn't what he thought. As the realization hit him, he jumped out of bed and started making phone calls to his grandmother and my sister Helen to find out what we should do. I ran across the hall to sit on the toilet, and to this day I can still picture him standing there in his undies, talking on the phone and slapping his forehead with the palm of his hand over and over again.

Soon we were on our way to the hospital, even though I was not having any pains. About ten minutes after we got to the hospital, the pains started, and there was none of this nonsense of pains every so many minutes. Once they started, they were nonstop and hurt like hell. In short order, I was in the delivery room pushing with all my might, and nothing was happening. They kept putting a mask over my face, but I wasn't getting any relief. Then I felt them cutting me. A vision of a butcher knife cutting raw meat came into my mind, and I screamed as hard as I could. That was the last thing I remembered until later that day. Bradley Alexander Gagnon was born at 5:12 AM, weighing in at eight pounds thirteen ounces.

When I came to later in the day, the first thing I did was feel my stomach. It felt soft like rising bread dough, so I knew the baby had been born. When I tried to ask someone about it, no one seemed to know anything. Finally, a nurse told me that I had a boy, one of nine babies born through the night. Eight of them had been males. I guess it had been a pretty busy night for the Oshawa General Hospital! Also, when I came to I could hardly speak because my throat was really sore, and I just figured it was from screaming. About a year later, Bruce confessed that after Brad was born one of the nurses had asked him to try to get the tube out of my mouth. Apparently, I had my teeth clamped around it pretty tightly, and, thinking it was only just inside my mouth, Bruce gave a good yank. When he managed to pull it free, the tube was much longer than he had anticipated. Feeling guilty, he had been afraid to tell me why I had such a sore throat.

I also had thirty-six stitches because Brad had what was considered a big head. Bruce's grandmother took great pride in letting me know that big heads ran in the Gagnon and Cameron families. At the end of my pregnancy, I weighed 128 pounds, and the day after Brad was born, I was back down to 112 pounds, so this was a good size baby.

Brad had reddish blond hair and was a very healthy baby. He was a good sleeper right from the start. Back then, Lois wasn't married yet, so, whenever one of us had a baby, she would take a week's holiday and come and stay with us to help us out. She stayed with us in our little three-room basement apartment and slept on the pullout chesterfield in the living room. She and Bruce pampered me and decided they would do all the tending to Brad.

The first night home, I was having a nice sleep when I was woken up by the two of them deciding whether or not to wake the baby. It was almost six in the morning, and he was still sleeping. I think that they did finally decide to get him up and make sure he was okay, or maybe they were just ready to play with him. Either way, with the two of them fussing over him all week, I certainly didn't have to worry whether he was being looked after.

Bruce was still off work and in and out of the hospital, so our finances were not good. Consequently, when Brad was only about five weeks old, I started looking for a job. I got one right away at a factory in Ajax that made surgical gloves. My job was in the inspection department, and I spent eight hours a day blowing up surgical gloves on an air machine and checking them for pinholes, lumps of rubber, and stuff like that. The first week I was blowing up gloves in my sleep every night, but it was extra money coming in and I was fortunate that we had good friends who could babysit whenever Bruce wasn't able to.

About two weeks after I started working, we found out that Bruce's grandmother was hosting a surprise baby shower for us. Two days before the party, Bruce was driving to a physiotherapy appointment with Brad lying on the front seat beside him. There weren't car seats for small babies at that point. Some guy made a left-hand turn in front of him, and our car was totaled. Bruce's main concern was Brad, and he immediately handed Brad and his wallet to one of the witnesses at the scene and asked him to take Brad to the hospital, which the other guy did. Bruce stayed at the scene of the accident until everything was arranged and then went to the hospital. Fortunately, Brad was fine. The bad news was that we no longer had a vehicle. Bruce's best friend Richard (yes, the same one from the A&W) came to pick me up at work and let me know what was going on and that everyone was okay.

When Friday came, we still did not have another vehicle, so Bruce's cousin and his girlfriend gave us a ride to the party. On the way, Bruce was commenting that because he didn't have to drive, he would able to drink as much as he wanted to. When we got to the party, that's exactly what he proceeded to do. He spent the time with his buddies, and I opened all the gifts by myself. I was definitely feeling abandoned but tried to hide it as much as I could. I felt that everyone was judging me and thinking that I mustn't be a very good wife or else my husband would be at my side helping me out! By the end of the night, Bruce was very drunk, and I was very humiliated. Because it was our party, we had to stay until everyone had left, and this made it an extremely long night. When everyone had gone, I guess Bruce decided that he had some atoning to do, so he started turning on the charm with his grandmother. He also decided that he would go and sit beside her. I have no idea where his mind was, but he sat down beside her with no chair in sight.

He went ass over teakettle, and, for the first and only time in my life, I literally saw red. Everything faded away except the rage that I was feeling. I really didn't care what anyone thought at this point. I ranted and raved at him, which was useless with the state he was in, and finally I cooled down enough to packed everything up to go home. Bruce still couldn't see where he had done anything wrong, and all the way home he kept talking like everything was fine. When we got back to the apartment, we had one hell of a fight, probably the worst in our thirty-eight years of marriage. I was determined to leave, but he sat on the floor in front of the door all night so that I couldn't. I had cooled down somewhat by the next morning, and Bruce was beginning to see his responsibility in what had happened. We managed to sort things out and decided to see how things would go. The fight had also served the purpose of getting us kicked out of our first apartment, and we had to begin looking for another place to live. We found a two-bedroom apartment and moved there in April of 1972.

I continued working at my job for almost a year. At first it wasn't too bad, but with everything else that was going on with a new baby, Bruce in and out of the hospital, and our financial future not looking good, things began to wear on me. At that time there were no disposable diapers, and quite often after I came home I had to do laundry in an old wringer washer. We didn't have a dryer, so everything had to be hung out and brought in later. It's a good thing I had all that experience from growing up on a farm!

My immediate family also underwent a number of changes during this period. Bruce likes to claim the responsibility of getting his best friend Richard together with Mona, and the next thing we knew Richard had became our brother-in-law. Eventually, they had three great kids: Ryan, Jillian, and Jonathon. Betty married Ken, and they had two boys: Scott and Steven. Helen had baby number four, and, being married to Tom and obviously obsessed with the letter 'T' named her kids Terry, Tammy, Tracy and Tricia. Lois waited and married Karl after the rest of us were married and settled down. They had two girls together: Karla and Becky. In a few short years, all five sisters and Carl got married and started families. We were often together, and the kids were so close in age that they were oftentimes more like siblings than cousins.

Chapter 16
Me ... Fired? Okay, We'll Have Another Baby

When summer came that year, my job at the factory became almost unbearable. At one point, it was 128 degrees in the plant where we were working. Everyone complained of the heat, and, although we had a union, they were totally useless. Finally, one day when we were in the cafeteria and everyone was complaining, we came up with the idea that if we all walked out, the company would have no choice but to do something about fixing the air conditioning. I volunteered to be the one to stand up at eleven o'clock, and then everyone agreed that at my signal, they would stand up with me and we would all walk out.

Well, there were twenty-eight of us working in that department, and, when I stood up at the assigned time, two others stood up with me. Obviously, someone must have told management what we were planning, because, as soon as I stood up, our union rep and the management greeted me. The three of us who stood up were taken into the office and invited to resign because we were troublemakers and not welcome there anymore. In one way it was okay, because I was not feeling well. My family doctor had already told me that I had not yet regained my health from having the baby and that it would be a good idea to find work that was less stressful. All the same, I wanted to make a difference before I walked away.

Later on, when I spoke to some of the other employees and asked why they backed out, they told me they knew there was a risk of losing their jobs and they weren't willing to take the chance. I guess this was another lesson in trust, and, I came to the realization that a lot of times people will tell you what they think you want to hear and then do the complete opposite. Anyway, I was out of a job, and that was not good news.

I went back to my part-time job at the A&W and Bruce was able to return to work, so things began to look up a bit. The Worker's Compensation Board told Bruce that his back problems would be a permanent thing, and they allowed him back to work on light duty and gave him a pension of $68 a month. I think he was just happy to be able to get back to work and be done with the hospital, doctors, and all the tests and physiotherapy.

Once Bruce was back to work, some of my own health problems seemed to worsen. My family doctor attributed them to the birth control pill, so we began thinking that maybe we would like another baby. I figured that Brad was an easy child, so how much harder could another one be? How naive I was. I also decided that it might be a good idea to get a little more education so that I could get a better job. I enrolled in a program that was paid for by Unemployment. They would pay me to go back to school and take a secretarial course. It wasn't a lot of money, but it did help. I went to school full-time for the forty-week course. By the time I finished it, I was about six months pregnant. No one really wanted to hire me for just a few months, so I started babysitting at home to make some extra money.

Our best friends, George and Linda, an English couple who had come to Canada just after they were married, had a little girl, Joanne, who was a few months older than Brad. We were together a lot, and Linda had babysat for Brad while I was working. They were our first close adult friends, and we did almost everything together. When it was time for me to go to the hospital for our second child, we dropped Brad off with them, and away we went full of excitement and anticipation.

This time around, everything was very different. I was the only one on the maternity ward, and the pains were few and far between, I didn't want any type of anesthetic unless it was absolutely necessary. By this time, the hospitals were finally allowing the fathers to be present at the birth, and Bruce was eager to be a part of it. I went into the hospital at about one in the morning, and, with this child taking her time, we spent the night entertaining each other. Bruce was constantly checking the baby's heart rate and playing the comedian. I don't know if it was because he was nervous or just trying to pass the time, but finally, at about eight thirty in the morning, it was time to go to the delivery room.

Bruce was sent off by the nurses to gown up. As I was going into the delivery room, I heard the nurses laughing, and I later found out that Bruce had gone into the doctor's changing room and had put on one of their gowns and caps. Needless to say, he was sent back to change, and, by the time he got to the door of the delivery room, he could hear a baby crying. Andrea Laura Jean Gagnon popped into this world at 8:52 on the morning of November 19, 1973, weighing in at six pounds, twelve ounces. I had a perfect delivery without drugs, and she was absolutely perfect and beautiful—a wonderful gift just two days before our third anniversary. Both Bruce and I were overwhelmed and full of joyful tears. We now had a boy and a girl. What more could we possibly want in life?

Brad was totally enthralled with his new baby sister, and it was a good thing that he could sleep through anything because she was awake the majority of the time. I tried to breast-feed for the first month but finally had to give it up because Andrea was not taking to it very well. We put her on formula and spent the next several months trying one brand after another to get her to settle down. At one point, I think out of frustration, the doctor recommended that we put some vodka in her formula to see if that would settle her down so she would sleep. It didn't work, and she was more hyperactive than ever. Two years later and after all kinds of testing and sleepless nights, the doctors determined that she was allergic to three out of the four sugars found in foods. In the meantime, Bruce and I took care of her in shifts. We were lucky if she slept two hours a day, and there were times, even with our vigilant attitude, that we fell asleep on the job and suffered the consequences, which you'll hear more about shortly.

After Andrea was born, we decided to settle down and buy a house. At that time condominiums were making their debut in Oshawa as an affordable alternative to the traditional single-family home. Our saving grace was that there were no computers yet, and we were able to do a little manipulation to get what we wanted. As we had not been able to save any money up to this point, we went to a finance company and borrowed $2000. The payment was $63 a month, which we figured could be paid out of Bruce's Worker Compensation pension. So we got our down payment and headed off to apply for a mortgage. We didn't tell them about the loan or the pension, and at that time there was no way for them to check. We managed to qualify for the mortgage, and, in the spring of 1974, we moved into our first home. We paid $28,000 for it, and our mortgage, taxes, and maintenance fee, which included everything except our telephone, was $301 a month. It was a struggle, but we were determined to make it work. Bruce and I both wanted me to be a stay-at-home mom, and, with Andrea being such a handful, it would have been almost impossible for me to work. It was hard for Bruce too because he would give me a break and then go off to work, sometimes with very little sleep.

One time, he woke me up to tell me that he was leaving for work and I was so tired that I fell back to sleep. When I woke up and went to check on Andrea, she had managed to get out of her room and had gone into the bathroom and created total chaos. My makeup was everywhere. She had tried to put it on herself, and her little face was covered in lipstick, powder, eyeliner, mascara, and eye shadow. She had created a total mess with shampoo and cleaning supplies and had pulled almost everything out of the vanity under the sink. I don't think there was a square inch of the bathroom that escaped intact. I totally lost it and started screaming and yelling like a banshee. Fortunately, our neighbor Maxine came running from next door, took one look, and took control. She helped to settle me down and get the mess cleaned up. I don't know what I would have done if she had not been there for me that day.

Andrea was as smart as she was destructive. At less than a year old she could get out of her crib and her room. Her crib was one that my Uncle Bob had for his girls. Uncle Bob or Bobby as I called him was my biological mother's brother and we became acquainted with him and his wife, Lynn, when they were living in Oshawa. When he offered us the crib, I jumped at the chance of something that was connected to my biological roots. It was a beautiful chrome crib that could be unlocked from its stationery position so it could be rocked. Keep in mind that there were also no safety guidelines for cribs like there are now.

Anyway, Andrea figured out very early on that she could do lots of things with this crib. Because it was on casters, she could rock it around the room and gain access to things on top of the dressers and to the edges of the wallpaper, so she could peel the paper off the walls. She could also jump in the crib and manipulate it so that she could unhook the mattress from the frame. She would then slide down the mattress and right out onto the floor.

Once free of the confined space of the crib, she would wreak havoc throughout her room. It was not unusual to find everything in her room in disarray. Because of this, we were cautious of what we left in her room. To keep her safe if she got out of the crib, we installed doorknob covers that just spin around so she could not open the door. These were soft plastic ones, not the hard plastic that's available today. Well, she even figured that one out. After the bathroom escapade, I wanted to know how she had gotten out of her room, so I went into her room with her, closed the door, and just sat on the floor and watched her for a while. It didn't take long until she went over to the door, put both of her hands on the door handle, and started walking up the door with her feet. This provided her with enough pressure on the door handle to turn the handle and open the door. So much for child proofing!

Chapter 17
The Hospital in the Big City

When I was about five months pregnant with Andrea, I developed psoriasis on my elbows. By the time she was six months old, it had spread to almost all of the joint areas in my body. My arms, legs, and head were covered with it, and it seemed that I was constantly at the doctor's office trying to find some miracle cure to tame it. I went to see a specialist, and, after trying many different drugs, creams, and ointments, he thought I might benefit from being in the hospital, where I could undergo the heavy tar treatments combined with light therapy. I was in St. Michael's Hospital in Toronto for almost a month while Bruce took time off work to stay with the kids. He managed to get up and see me each weekend, but it was a tough time for both of us.

At that time, Toronto was still the big, dangerous city to me, and, the night before I was to be admitted, I dreamed that the hospital had made a mistake when they admitted me and put me in the crazy ward instead. That was one of the most frightening dreams I have ever had, and it stayed with me when I went to the hospital to be checked in. I was sure that I was going to disappear into the nether regions of this giant place, never to be seen or heard from again. Needless to say, that's not what happened, and my experience over the next month was nothing like my dream—thank you, God.

Once I was admitted and taken to my room, the staff immediately began getting me into treatment. They brought me this thick, white ointment to put on my scalp, because it was almost raw from the psoriasis. The nurse warned me not to put it on my skin, just my scalp, but didn't tell me why. I had a huge spot of psoriasis right in the middle of my forehead, and, after the cream on my scalp, I thought, "I'll just put a little here on my forehead. That's close to my scalp, and no one will ever know that I did it." I used the heavy, coal tar on the rest of my body and got myself all wrapped up and into bed. When I woke up the next morning and looked in the mirror, there in the middle of my forehead was this big purple spot. I spent the day covered in guilt for getting caught doing something I wasn't supposed to have done!

I should have known better, because years ago, when I was fairly young, Betty had had psoriasis, and Daddy went to the drugstore and asked the pharmacist to mix up an ointment with potassium permanganate in it. It was a white cream that turned purple once it was on the skin. The reason I remembered this incident is because the family had a good laugh over Daddy getting the cream. Apparently, this cream was mostly used for venereal disease, and, when Daddy had asked for it, the pharmacist started questioning which of his daughters he was getting it for. Unfortunately, remembering this after the fact didn't help me in the least.

During the time I was in the hospital, I missed Andrea's first birthday and our fourth anniversary. Bruce was able to come up and spend the day with me to celebrate our anniversary, and I even got a day pass so that we could go out into downtown Toronto.

As the weeks went by, it became extremely difficult for Bruce to keep things going, and he would call me at night and fill me in on what was happening at home. I could tell that he was not coping as well as he let on, and, consequently, I began to worry. Because stress plays a huge role in psoriasis, mine began to get worse again. Finally, my doctor told me that I could probably do better by being at home and released me. Thus started twenty years of wearing long-sleeve shirts and long pants so that others couldn't see my horrible skin. I continued going to specialists until one almost killed me and then I just gave up and accepted the fact that I would be disfigured and ugly like this for the rest of my life.

I had tried almost everything to get my skin better. I went to a chiropractor who swore he could cure me by having me come in three times a week and get connected to a machine that would balance my "poles." I also had to drink this horrible, murky purple tea that tasted like it had been strained through somebody's dirty socks. After about three months of this, when I went in one day. the doctor had his shirtsleeves rolled up, and there he was, also covered in psoriasis.

I made the rounds for years, trying everything to get rid of the psoriasis. One of the skin specialists that I went to see put me on treatments of methotrexate. When I asked what it was, he ignored my question. I had earlier been conditioned to do as the doctor said, so I allowed him to experiment on me. I would go into his office and have needles inserted in all the areas where the psoriasis was, and the next week I would sit in his office and swallow ten tiny, white pills.

After a few months of this, I had lost quite a bit of weight and was feeling nauseous all the time. When I mentioned this to him, he told me not to worry, that it wasn't caused by the medication I was taking. Finally, I went to my family doctor. When I told him about the medication that the specialist had me on, he immediately called another skin specialist a couple of floors up. That doctor wanted to see me immediately. This other doctor went up one side of me and down the other, until I felt like the stupidest person on Earth. He told me in no uncertain terms that I should have been having blood tests all along. He explained that the symptoms I was experiencing were a side effect of the medication and that if I didn't stop taking it immediately I would become a hell of a lot sicker. I think this was the straw that broke the camel's back. I finally started to get that doctors don't know everything and maybe I should just stay as far away from them as much as I could. To this day, I have never gone back to a skin specialist. Instead, I put cream on my skin when it bothered me too much, wore long sleeves and long pants, and did my best to come to terms with the fact that I was no longer an attractive human being.

This went on for about twenty-two years, and finally one day, I thought, "f—— it, I want to wear skirts and shorts and short sleeves," so I started to do that. At first I got comments almost everywhere I went. People asked me if I had been in a car accident, if I had gotten burned, or even if I had contracted some disease from a foreign country. The one time I attempted to go swimming with Bruce and the kids at a family swim day, I got asked to leave the pool because they couldn't take my word that what I had was not contagious. I would read about psoriasis whenever I could find information and eventually decided to take matters into my own hands. I started taking flaxseed oil, alternating with fish oils. I was a little more cautious with the foods that I was eating, and, within a year, my psoriasis had faded to less than half of the areas. I also found that tanning helped, and, within two to three years, my skin had cleared to about 90 percent of what it was. That has remained to this day, and anyone meeting me today would only see a few patches of dry skin.

Chapter 18
Opportunity Comes Knocking

Bruce and I both wanted me to be a stay-at-home mom, but, in order to do this, we were going to have to find another source of income. We both wanted more out of life, and, with two children to raise, we understood that one income as great as it was, was not going to allow us much leeway.

Condominiums were a new concept in our area, and shortly after we moved in, the builder was looking for a superintendent to clean the hallways and maintain the grounds. The pay was $450 a month, which was nothing to sneeze at. Bruce applied for the job, but, with his recent history of back problems from GM, they wouldn't even consider him. Another resident got the position and hired Bruce to do the work for him at a reduced rate. Still, we were happy because we made enough money to cover our mortgage and maintenance fee. Then, one day, Gerry Armstrong, the owner/builder of our condominium, came in and saw Bruce working. When he found out what was going on and what a good job Bruce was doing, he took the job from the other guy and made Bruce the superintendent with the full amount of pay. The only part of the job that we hadn't been doing was cleaning and mopping the hallways twice a week. This became my part of the job, and, although I hated every minute of it, I did it without complaint because of the extra income. I also had the advantage of being able to watch my kids as I worked. This arrangement lasted for two years until a better offer came along.

Our two years at our first townhouse were typical for first-time homebuyers with small children. It provided for new friendships for both us as parents as well as our children, and we had a lot of fun times.

The kids had a safe place to play most of the time, yet there were some challenges. One day, when Andrea was about two years old, we were getting ready to go out and I had her all dressed up. A few of the older kids in the complex asked if they could take her to the playground until we were ready to leave. I gave my consent and was about to leave the house five minutes later when the kids showed up on our doorstep. Andrea's face was bleeding like crazy. I put a cold wet cloth on it and immediately headed to urgent care. When we got there, the doctor told me that the cut below her eye was going to require stitches.

Because Andrea was unsure of what was going on, she was quiet and did as she was told for a change. She lay there on the table without saying a word, just watching out of the corner of her eye as the doctor started sewing her up. She must have unnerved the doctor a bit, because after the second stitch went in, he looked at her and said, "You can say ouch if you want to." Andrea figured that that was what she was supposed to say, because for the next four stitches, every time he put the needle in, she would look at him and say "ouch." She didn't raise her voice or anything; she just said the words.

Another time, we came out into the parking lot one morning and someone had spray-painted our car. We weren't living in the best neighborhood, and Bruce's efforts to keep our little complex nice created problems with some of the kids in the community. For the most part, he tried to keep the kids on his side, but there was some resentment that sometimes manifested into property damage.

Without any regrets, we accepted a better offer from our superintendent employer, Armstrong Homes. The property manager came to see us one day and told us that the company was building a new condominium in another area and needed a superintendent to look after it. There was a pay increase, and we would have first pick on which unit we wanted. The best part was that there would not be hallways to sweep and mop a couple of times a week. We chose our unit and moved in April the following year. We felt that we were really doing well. These units had garages, dining rooms, two bathrooms, and a swimming pool. It was a perfect setting for our kids to grow up safely with good schools nearby, and our new home was in an older, well-established neighborhood. What more could we want?

Even though this property was larger and more work to maintain, it provided a good income that still allowed me to stay home with the kids. Life was good, and we made friendships that have endured to this day. One of the flaws of having the superintendent's job was that we had to rely on a contractor to come in and plow the roadways in the wintertime. Sometimes they wouldn't show up until the day after a heavy snow, and, after a few frustrating winters, Bruce decided he could do a better job than these contractors, so he bought an old blazer, put a plow on it, and started snowplowing. Even though he was still working at GM and working long hours when it snowed, it was a good move on his part.

After we had been in our new place for a couple of years, the builder, who was also the property manager, once again approached us to let us know that the condominium industry was changing. There would no longer be superintendents, and contractors would be hired instead. These contractors would do all of the work. It was the beginning of a whole new phase in our lives. We registered our business, set up an office, and began to learn everything we could about business. We even took a human relations course at the local college to learn how to deal with customers and potential employees. We began by maintaining properties that Armstrong Homes owned and gradually built the company into a full-time enterprise. There were a lot of obstacles to overcome. In those early years before the kids were in school, it was common for Bruce to come home from the night shift at GM at 2:30 in the morning, and we would load the sleeping children into the truck. I would drive as Bruce shoveled salt onto the roadways from the back of the truck. It was a great learning experience, and here we are thirty-five years later, still doing well and very proud of what we have built.

When we had been in business a few years and were doing quite well with a few employees, it became apparent that Bruce could not keep up the pace of a full-time job plus the business, so we had to make a decision. One of them had to go. Bruce had been unhappy at GM almost from the beginning because of the monotony of line working, but the money and the benefits package with a full pension were excellent. On the other hand, he loved the outdoor work of landscaping and maintenance, but there was no guarantee of work, no benefits, and no pension. After much deliberation, he opted for quitting GM. When he told his foreman that he was leaving, his foreman was supportive but did not want him to act too hastily, so he suggested that Bruce take a thirty-day leave of absence to see how things worked out. Bruce did this, and, at the end of the thirty days, made the decision to stay at GM for the next month until he had his ten years of service completed. By doing this, he would be entitled to collect a partial pension at retirement. However, the day that he returned to work after his leave of absence, he was awarded four winter contracts, and Bruce took that as a sign that everything would be okay to move forward with the business. He promptly quit his job at GM—less than a month shy of his ten years of service.

Business-wise, the years were pretty good to us. We were able to make a decent living, and I sometimes worked part-time to bring in a little extra income. Meanwhile, the kids started school, and life seemed to be normal.

Chapter 19
What Do You Do with a Rolls Royce?

Some things that happen in your life have such an impact that you can close your eyes years later and recall them as if they happened yesterday. One of those times for us was in late October in the late 1970s. We had bought a ticket for the Juvenile Diabetes Foundation Draw. The tickets were $100 each, but, because Bruce's mom had been diagnosed with diabetes shortly before that, we figured it was a good way to donate to the cause and possibly get something in return. These types of draws were not commonplace in those years and it was a lot of money, but we bought the ticket anyway. The draw was to take place at the Inn on the Park in Toronto, and, when we found out that friends had tickets as well, we all decided to go together. It's interesting to note that this friend was also our lawyer, whom I'd known since my A&W days, and is still our lawyer today.

We headed up to the draw with the plan of having a nice evening out. It started out as an okay evening. At first we paid attention, but, as our numbers weren't coming up, we kind of lost interest in the proceedings. All of a sudden, I heard the number 729 being called. Bruce didn't believe that they had called our number, so he went to check. Sure enough, it was one of the last ten numbers to be called. Then the fun began.

Out of the final ten, seven numbers were eliminated. Ours was one of the three left, which meant that the three remaining

Hooray, we're Rolls-rich!

87

numbers could agree to split the prize of a Rolls Royce or $60,000. If the last three couldn't agree, then there would be elimination and the last two could agree to split or go for the whole thing.

Only two out of the three of us with tickets were there, so the third person had to be contacted to find out their decision. When that person wasn't available by phone, elimination was done, and, by sheer chance, the person eliminated was the absentee. This left one other couple and us to make a decision. It wasn't much of a decision though, because, if we shared, we both won. It was either split the $60,000 or possibly go home with a $20 food voucher. We agreed to split, and, for the next few hours and well into the night, we were invited to a private suite for champagne and celebration. We were given a check for $30,000, interviewed by the newspapers, and had our picture taken numerous times. The next day our picture was in all of the Toronto and Durham newspapers, and the *Toronto Star* even printed that, if we had proceeded to the final elimination, Bruce and I would have taken the entire $60,000.

Of course, we called home immediately to let our families share in the good news. I think we all celebrated for the next twenty-four hours. It was a once-in-a-lifetime experience, and now when we see someone who is excited because they have won the lottery, we have an inkling of how they are feeling. We took the money and invested in a cottage that was on a lake not far from Oshawa. The advantage was that we would not have to drive far to get there.

Long before we had won the money or bought the cottage, we had purchased off-road motorcycles for me, Brad, and Bruce. Bruce's brother and his wife, Glen and Sheree, had also bought bikes, and we used to go out on Sundays to a place called the Ridges and go biking for the day. It was a lot of fun, and I would take Andrea on the back of my bike. When Andrea was about five years old, we decided it was time for Brad to move to a bigger bike and Andrea could take over his. So one Sunday we decided it was time for her to learn how to ride. Bruce and Glen gave her the instructions on driving and had her riding back and forth between them, while she learned to change gears, brake, and all the other necessary details. Andrea was very smart, and within no time she had complete confidence. She was so confident that she wanted to show us how good she was. She pulled away from Bruce, heading toward Glen, and decided to open up the gas. By the time she got to Glen, she was going full throttle. Glen was a bit worried, so he tried to stop her so she wouldn't hurt herself. As she came toward him, he grabbed the handlebars. She was going so fast that Glen, Andrea, and the bike did a full circle in the air, landing pretty hard. Andrea thought this was great fun, but, after some chastising from both her dad and her uncle, she agreed to be more cautious. It didn't deter her much, though, and she took to bike riding very naturally. This was our Andrea!

The cottage offered great opportunities with the bikes, and quite often we would take off on Sunday mornings and go out riding for a few hours. It was great family time. However, Bruce did pull a stunt that raised Brad's ire. We were at the cottage, and Brad had just gotten his new bike that week. Bruce and Glen had hoisted a few pints and were in a betting mood. Glen bet Bruce ten bucks that he couldn't ride Brad's bike off the end of the dock and into the lake. Never one to let a challenge pass him by, Bruce took the bet and off he went. What he didn't account for was the extremely muddy bottom of Lake Scugog. When he went off the end of the dock, he planned on immediately getting the bike back up on the dock, but instead the bike sunk deep into the mud. It was a good hour before they managed to get the bike back onto land. They spent much of the rest of the weekend trying to get the mud out of the bike and trying to get Brad to talk to them again. In the end, they had to bring it home and give it a complete overhaul to get it going.

There was always something going on at the cottage, and, because we were so close to Oshawa, we always had lots of company. The kids even had a vegetable garden out back, and we would pull weeds and clean it up on Friday nights while Bruce cut the grass. Some of our employees would even come up with their families and go waterskiing and to relax for the day. It was a lot of fun, but also a lot of work. After a few years, I had had enough. It seemed that every Friday I would spend the day grocery shopping and loading the car to go to the cottage. Then, when we got there on Friday night, it was unpacking everything and making up the beds while Bruce got the outside work done. Then Saturday and Sunday we would entertain, only to wake up on Sunday and reverse all of the work: cleaning everything and packing the car up again to go home. Bruce was beginning to feel the same way, so we decided to sell the cottage and buy a boat instead.

The boat was twenty-eight feet long with a fly bridge and slept six people. We used sleeping bags instead of sheets, and the kids would each bring a friend for the weekend. We thoroughly enjoyed it. It was peaceful to be on the water, and even our dog Snoopy loved it. That worked for a while until the kids got to the point where they had part-time jobs and would rather stay in town with their friends to go to dances and things on Friday and Saturday nights. The last year that we had the boat, we were only on it three times. It didn't make sense to keep it any longer. The cost of maintenance and docking the boat was quite expensive, so we decided to sell it and spend our weekends at home, where we could keep an eye on what the kids were up to.

Another interesting thing happened during this same period in our lives. My biological mother, or as we called her, Mother Pauline, had always been in sporadic contact with us. When Monie and I were very young, she would come maybe once a year to visit us. Monie was always leery of her and didn't really want anything to do with her, but I was always willing to greet her and accepted her in any way that I could. She would always send us birthday cards that had us two years older than we actually were. For example, when I was five, my card said, "Happy Birthday, 7-year-old," and so on. She had come to Oshawa to visit me once after I moved in with Reg and Brenda and had attended both Mona's and my weddings. Mother Pauline lived up in Rouyn, Quebec, so other than her occasional visit to Oshawa, our only contact was by writing letters. Bruce and I had gone up to visit her when Brad was a baby, and I had briefly met her other four sons. There were twin boys, Emile and Michel, John Paul, and Andre.

In 1977 Bruce and I had purchased our first new vehicle, which was a truck, and had put a camper on the back of it. We thought it would be a great opportunity to go up north and visit her, which we did. We had a good visit with her and the only son living at home at that time was Andre, who was fifteen years old. John Paul had enlisted in the armed forces and was stationed in Germany. I have no idea where the twins were.

When we left Rouyn to come home, Mother Pauline sent Andre with us to visit for a few weeks until school started. It was a good visit because we tried to do different things like going to the CNE with him, but I think that a fifteen-year-old boy who barely knew the people he was with was not too impressed. I never did see Andre again. He was killed in a car crash years later in the early nineties.

Emile showed up one time, driving an old van with a parrot for a companion. He left the bird with us for a few days while he went to visit an aunt who lived about an hour away. When he returned, he came into the family room, sat down, and lit up a joint. As our kids were at a pretty impressionable age, I was upset, and the visit got cut short. To this day, I have not seen or heard from him again.

Having children of my own, I began to think that I would like to find out more information about my father. I wrote a letter to Mother Pauline and asked about him. I did not hear anything for six years, and then one day a curt letter came from her. Included was a copy of her marriage certificate, which was dated just a few days before I was born.

This got me thinking, so I wrote back to her and told her that I didn't care about the circumstances—I just wanted the truth. Again, it was a while before I received her return letter. It confirmed my suspicions about my grandfather's role in my conception. At this point, I didn't know whether to believe her because I wasn't sure how truthful she was being with me, so I just let the matter rest. I didn't hear from her again until 1986.

In 1986 John Paul was home from the armed forces and living in Rouyn with his German wife, Ilona. As job prospects were not the best at that time, Mother Pauline suggested that they come to Oshawa to see if they could find work. They arrived on our doorstep on Easter Sunday and stayed with us for a month while John Paul looked for work. Ilona was eight months pregnant with their first child, Christine. Keep in mind that I had only seen John Paul once before in my life, and he had been a child at that time. Ilona spoke quite a bit of English, but there was still somewhat of a language barrier. Although it was difficult for all of us, we managed to muster through. John Paul got a job right away, and within a month they had found a place to live and settled in quite nicely.

Not too long after that, my mother decided that she might like to move to Oshawa. I think that she was under the impression that somehow we could mend fences and become close, but my guard was up. Although I was willing to visit with her, I was not about to become best friends. She lived in Oshawa for a year and then decided to move back to Quebec, but continued to be part of John Paul and Ilona's life for a while longer.

A few years after John Paul and Ilona moved to Oshawa, they invited Mother Pauline's mom, Grandma Brunette, from Belleville up to visit them. I had seen her once when I was about six years old when Monie and I were visiting with Daddy's sister, Aunt Leona. Back then, Grandma Brunette had come to Aunt Leona's to pick up Monie and me and had taken us out for the day and then back to her house for supper. The only thing I remember about that day was that she bought us banana splits (which I thought were really gross) and then going to her house with her two youngest children, who were only a year or two older than Mona and I. We sitting at the table eating supper when one of the kids said something funny. We all started giggling. All of a sudden, Grandpa Brunette said something to Grandma, and the next thing we knew we were banished from the room and sent to a bedroom. That was the last I had seen or heard from her until her visit to John Paul and Ilona's.

I went to meet her again at John Paul and Ilona's apartment, and at first she thought I was just a neighbor or a friend who had dropped by for a visit. When she realized who I was, she immediately wanted to form a relationship and become part of our lives. At first, I was open to this, and set about getting to know her. I wanted to find out more of the circumstances surrounding my birth and the first eighteen months of my life. I did get to know her quite well and had her up for weekly visits a couple of time a year.

As often as I could, I would try to turn the conversation to my mother and Grandpa. Most of those times, she would either ignore my questions or deflect the conversation by telling me about her relationship with Pauline. One time she almost admitted that it might be true, but that was as far as I got with her. She and my mother had not spoken for a number of years at that time, and to my knowledge they never spoke again.

My relationship with Grandma Brunette was a cautious one at best. I could quickly see that she was self-centered, and many times when she was visiting, she would become agitated and jealous when other members of my family or our friends would drop by. One day my neighbor was over having coffee with us, and Grandma said to her, "Don't you think it's time you went home now?" I was furious that she would dare to pull a stunt like that in my home.

When Grandma was at home in Belleville, one of her other daughters who lived not too far from her looked after her needs much of the time. Although Grandma lived on her own in a senior's apartment in Belleville, as she got older she began having a harder time being on her own, so she began to look for alternative living arrangements. She talked about moving in with us. At that time we had renovated our current house; it had no stairs and was easily accessible for anyone with a handicap. Even though I had the distinction of being her firstborn grandchild and could have afforded to have her live with us, I was not willing to consider it. I really did not have any emotional attachment to her, and there was no way I was going to have anyone live with us. Bruce and I had been through this exact same scenario years ago with his grandmother, and we had both agreed at that time that we liked our privacy and that we were not willing to jeopardize our relationship by allowing someone to come between us. In both of these cases, we were dealing with demanding and difficult people. Grandma finally made the decision to live with another granddaughter of hers in Montreal and lived there until she died during the big ice storm in 1998.

During this time of getting to know some of my biological family, I did a hell of a lot of thinking. I came to the conclusion that it is not my place to judge any of them or their actions. I did not feel any ill will toward any of them; however, for the most part, I had no wish to get to know them better either. John Paul and Ilona have become part of our lives over the years, and it's more like he's also been adopted into my family. He and his family are a part of our Thanksgivings and Christmases, and it really wouldn't be the same without them now.

Michel, Emile's twin, started coming to visit John Paul a couple of years ago and for the past few years has also been a part of our Thanksgiving celebration. I am getting to know him and his wife and hope that the relationship will continue to grow for many years to come. There is still the one other brother who was given up for adoption in 1955. Do I want to get to know him? I don't know. Sometimes you worry about opening doors that can't be closed.

Chapter 20
Teenagers Are Not Fun

When I said we needed to keep an eye on what the kids were up to, I certainly wasn't joking. It seemed that having Bruce and I for parents gave those kids a double whammy. We always said that we had no idea how to parent, because we really didn't have any role models. We were both fairly strict, which probably came from remembering all the antics that we had pulled when we were kids.

I had this notion that our family should be like the Cleaver family on the TV show *Leave It to Beaver*. If you don't remember the show, it was about a perfect family whose house was always spotless, there were family meals and home cooking every night, and the kids could be easily talked into seeing the error of their ways. (I was thirty-five before I got the idea out of my head that I was not going to be June Cleaver—all dressed up and looking perfect every moment of the day, even while doing housework!) I clung to the idea that every supper had to be at the dinner table, and everyone had to be there unless they were working. That holds true until this day, and, the odd time that we sit in front of the television to eat dinner, I feel as though I'm doing something really decadent.

Getting back on track, it seemed that our kids took turns getting into trouble. Until Andrea was about twelve years old and went to senior public school, she was an ideal student with an A average. Brad dominated those years. He did not like school from the beginning, and, unfortunately, his kindergarten teacher used new methods of teaching that allowed the students to grow at their own pace. There were no rules about participating, and, consequently, Brad spent most of that first year playing with cars and building blocks and not learning anything.

When he went into grade one, he again had a "modern" teacher. She believed in having kids learn to read by looking at the whole word rather than learning phonics and how to sound out words. By grade two Brad was lost, and, at the end of that year, the school wanted to hold him back. We came to an agreement that he would spend his next year in a grade two/three split class, but the damage was done.

He was constantly in trouble for something, never anything serious but he quickly got a reputation. When this happens, the child gets scrutinized even more closely. Don't get me wrong, he was no angel, and Bruce and I were from the old school way of learning that if the teacher said something was so, then it had to be the truth, sort of like the doctor thing. Whenever he got into trouble at school, he also had consequences at home. At times it seemed like an endless, vicious circle. We had always felt that kids who were involved in sports and extracurricular activities would be more likely to stay out of trouble, so we made sure the kids tried all kinds of things in hopes that they might find something they would take an avid interest in.

When Brad was in kindergarten, he came home one day and said he wanted to join Beavers. We had no idea what that was and found out that it was a fairly new Boy Scout program. I informed Bruce that this was Dad territory and sent him off to sign Brad up. They came home signed up. Not only had they signed up, but they had also volunteered me to lead! I gracefully agreed to give it a try and started a volunteer program that was to last for fifteen years. Another father who started at the same time became a very good friend, and in some ways would have an impact on us for years to come.

The year before Andrea was to start kindergarten, she was bored silly at home, so I enrolled her in preschool. She absolutely loved it, and it was a perfect venue to get her started with her education.

We believed in allowing the kids to choose what they wanted to be involved in, and, over the next few years, they played baseball and soccer and took swimming lessons, skating lessons, and ceramic classes. Because I had to drive them to these activities, it only made sense to be a volunteer, so I became the scorekeeper or helped out in whatever capacity that I was capable.

Brad and Andrea were also enrolled in day camps when they were younger, and they later attended camps every summer until they were old enough to hold down part-time jobs. Even though Bruce and I couldn't take summer holidays, we didn't want the kids to go without a break. Both of them absolutely loved camp. I think they would have attended the entire summer if we would have let them. I still have letters that they wrote home from camp, and some of them are pretty entertaining.

Andrea also became a member of Brownies and Girl Guides. I wasn't willing to be a leader, so I served on the parent committee instead. Years later, Andrea told me that she was angry that I hadn't become a leader like I had with the Boy Scouts.

Chapter 21
Moving Again

In 1980 our five-year term was up with our mortgage, and mortgage rates had soared to 17 and 18 percent. The renewal amount of our mortgage combined with maintenance fees were quite high, so we thought it might be time to look for alternatives. We started checking out the real estate market and found a well-kept backsplit in an established area of the city. It wasn't far from where we were, so the kids could stay at their old school or transfer to another one that was a little closer. The owners were retiring and agreed to hold a mortgage for 13 percent. The house was twice the size of our townhouse, and our mortgage payment would be a couple of hundred dollars less than we were currently paying.

It was a great move at the right time, and the previous owners were very good to us. Our moving day was the end of June, but they let us come over early to plant flowers in the gardens and even let us put our new appliance in the garage. Because they were going to moved before that, they even gave us a key so that we could come in if we wanted to do any work first.

We moved in, and Brad immediately met a boy of his own age two doors down, but there wasn't anyone Andrea's age around. She spent the summer grumbling and wanting to go back to Park Square, our old townhouse, to be with her friends.

We decided to enroll the kids in another school and felt this might give Brad a fresh start. Maybe old habits die hard. It didn't take long for him to start getting into trouble there, either. He got caught smoking outside of school property. He got kicked out of school for getting involved in a snowball fight. It was a lot of minor things, and I thought that if I volunteered in the school a few days a week it might help. I thought my presence might make him think twice about acting up. This worked for a while, and in the meantime the school wanted to perform all sorts of tests on him. Still believing that the school was the authority and that we should be respectful and do what they wanted, we agreed. It was determined that he had ADHD and was sent to see a psychiatrist. This doctor put him on Ritalin and insisted on seeing him once a month. He was also diagnosed as a slow learner and moved to a special ed class. Talk about being stigmatized!

The Ritalin did its job very well. From Monday to Friday, while he was taking it, he was quiet and zombielike. On the weekends, he was his normal self again. It took awhile for us to realize that the doped-up Brad was not normal. It might be a lot more convenient for the teachers, but it sure as hell wasn't helping him learn anything. We finally started to smarten up. We weaned him off of it and decided to handle whatever happened. Afterward, he didn't seem to get in as much trouble at school but still was not doing well academically. We hired a tutor who helped somewhat, but Brad still didn't like school very much.

Outside of school, he still managed to find trouble, or else trouble found him. One year we decided to have a Christmas open house on the Sunday before Christmas. We were expecting about fifty to sixty people over the course of the afternoon, and, as I was getting everything ready in the morning, I came across something that didn't belong to him. I can't remember what it was, but, when confronted, he finally admitted that he had stolen it from Eaton's. Bruce and I were both livid and frightened. Because it was a Sunday, all the stores were closed, so we decided to put off doing anything until Monday. On Monday morning we called the police station for advice. They suggested that we bring him down and they would have a serious talk with him. We picked him up from school and went straight to the police station. I don't know what she said to him, but I think it had an effect. To my knowledge, he never stole anything after that.

Bruce and I felt that we must be missing something and that we desperately needed help. We made an appointment with our family doctor, and he recommended family counseling. We attended family counseling for a number of months, and the therapist recommended

Brad for a day program for troubled youths. The problem was that there was a waiting list, and it could take up to two years to get him in. In the meantime, he started grade seven at the senior public school and was up to his old antics again. He got kicked out of school for mouthing off to the teacher, fighting with other kids, and any number of things. We were constantly being called into the school for parent consultations. One time, he walked off the school grounds, stood on the public sidewalk, and lit up a cigarette. Again, he got kicked out of school. By this time, we were smartening up to the school system. Although we did not agree with Brad's smoking, he was not on school property and therefore no crime had been committed. Bruce tried this reasoning with the school's head group, which consisted of Brad's teacher, the vice principle, the principle, and the school counselor. When this didn't work, he went directly to the school trustees. That was on a Friday night, and, sure enough, Monday morning Brad was back in school. Because he didn't like school in the first place Bruce and I felt that being kicked out was not a hardship for him.

After this incident the school had a vendetta not only for Brad but for us as well. They constantly rode Brad's back and found fault with everything he did. Near the end of grade seven, they called us in and told us that they were going to fail him because his marks were on the borderline of passing and failing. We refused to let them do this and decided to take matters into our own hands. We had heard about a private school in Barrie on the Billis Estate, which was owned by Canadian Tire. We made an appointment and went up to talk to them about Brad attending summer school. Brad was very reluctant and agreed only after a lot of arguing and ultimatums. He started school the first week of July, and we could only visit on Sundays.

I didn't go up after the first week because life was so peaceful without having to worry about him. But when I went up the second week, I was pleasantly surprised. Brad fit into the program very well, and, with only twelve kids there, he got the extra attention he needed. They also had a reward program that he liked a lot. When his lessons and homework were finished, he was allowed to go to the stables and help out with cleaning and looking after the horses. This was something he really liked, so he worked hard to get as much time as he could in the stables. By the end of the summer, his marks had improved tremendously, and he was ready to settle down and get through grade eight so he could get into high school.

Bruce also thought that a hobby might be handy for him, so they went to a regional auction and bought a bunch of bicycles. Brad had always been interested in changing parts and fooling around with bikes, so they decided he could use some of the bikes for parts and fix others up and resell them. I gave up the garage, and they set up a workbench and all the tools that he would need to start his project. One day, he and Andrea and a few friends were out there, and, because I had one of my frequent migraines, I was laying down on the couch that backed on to the garage. I could faintly hear their voices out there. I was just laying there quietly when all of a sudden I heard the F word loud and clear. I was off that couch and out the door as quickly as I could. I sent the other kids home and ordered Brad and Andrea into the house. They knew they were in big trouble because one of them had sworn, and they were standing in front of me in the kitchen with guilty looks on their faces. I told them that I was going to wash their mouths out with soap. I wasn't serious. I just wanted them to say they wouldn't do it again, but to my surprise they accepted my threat. Andrea piped up, "Please, Mommy, use bar soap. It doesn't taste as bad." I was so taken aback that I had to turn away from them to keep from laughing. Finally I let them go with the threat that if I ever heard them say that word again, I would definitely do it. I don't know where Andrea got her information from, because we had never done that, but I guess some of her friends had told her which tasted better.

Brad seemed to start maturing and getting into less trouble, and it was a good thing because Andrea decided it was her turn to act up.

Chapter 22
Andrea Struggles to Be Independent

Brad started high school at a school that was more of a trade school than scholastic. He settled in quite nicely, worked as many hours as he could at his part-time job, and seemed to be finally growing up. There continued to be ongoing problems, but they became fewer and much more manageable at least from a parental point of view. Overall, it seemed as though he was finally maturing.

On the other hand, Andrea was starting grade seven at the senior public school. She was doing very well in the beginning, but being in an environment with about two hundred kids all the same age eventually presented some challenges for her. Perhaps because she had never been a problem at school we didn't see what was coming. It seemed as though all of a sudden she was developing an interest in boys and trying to be a grown-up. She started hanging around with a different crowd and began to buck authority. Her social life became more important than her educational life, and, for the next five years, Bruce and I were on a roller coaster ride of anger, frustration, denial, and every other emotion that a parent out of their league would experience. The following is from my diary in 1986, shortly before all the traumatic events with Andrea started:

> *Andrea is in grade 7 this year and really doing well. She is playing the clarinet and enjoys it. She has 4 pen pals and says her plans are to finish high school, go to Paris for 6 months, go to university, and become an obstetrician/gynecologist. Knowing her, she will fulfill her goals. She is a delight to have around most of the time. She chatters insistently, is very open about*

her life, and never fails to come up with outrageous stories. We do have our differences about clothes and makeup, but we both do some compromising and I think we have a pretty good relationship.

The problems started with little things, like her asking to stay overnight at a friend's place and then we would find out that she wasn't there at all, but was instead at another friend's house whose parents didn't mind that they were going out to parties. We tried to be fair but firm, and it didn't always work. One night, after I had double checked on a party that she was going to and the parents assured me that they would both be there to supervise, I got a call around one o'clock in the morning. The kids decided to go to a local gathering place in a field that they called Pipeland, and the parent had been afraid to tell them that they couldn't leave her house. Thank goodness she called me, but it still took us a couple of hours to find them.

Andrea's friends did not seem to have many of the same rules that she had, so she just decided to adopt theirs and to hell with ours. She was changing jobs constantly, lying about where she was and who she was with, and just seemed to have jumped on a path of self-destruction. She was caught stealing with a bunch of other kids at a shopping center and was charged by the police. I'm not sure if it was the stealing charge or some other infraction, but the one time when she had to go to court, she was sentenced to a youth detention center for a short time. We had been through so much with her that having her locked away in a safe facility gave us a breather. On Friday night, Brad was working the overnight shift at a gas station and, with Andrea in the safety of lockup, we decided at the last minute to attend a Christmas dance in Toronto. We even toyed with the idea of spending the night in a hotel just to be away from everything but then decided not to stay over. We got back from the dance around 1:00 AM and decided to bring Brad a hot coffee to warm him up. When we pulled in to the gas station, Brad was frantic. Andrea had escaped from the detention center and had called Bruce's brother Glen to come and get her. She and another girl had devised a plan and had managed to get away and make their way to Whitby. Because it was late November and very cold, she was freezing. The two of them had managed to escape but did not even have a coat or shoes to keep them warm. By the time we got to Glen's house, Andrea had managed to convince her uncle Glen that she was still the little angel that he remembered and that all the other adults in the world totally misunderstood her. She had Glen and Sheree convinced that she was the wronged one in all the shit that was going on.

We quickly set them straight, and then we had a talk with Andrea and told her that we had to take her back to the facility or else we could all be in serious trouble. It took awhile, but finally she came with us peacefully to the police station, where we handed her back into custody.

Somewhere during these trying times, Andrea met a guy named Terry from Jamaica who was nine years older than her. For some reason, he held a fascination for her that would almost destroy her and our family. By this time, Andrea was fourteen years old. Even though the age difference and the ages of Andrea and Terry were similar to what I had experienced as a teenager, that's where the comparisons end. Andrea had grown up to this point without ever having to take on the life experiences and responsibilities that I had. We had sheltered her and protected her as much as we could, maybe even too much.

Even now, thinking about what we went through over that next little while is difficult to remember. The following notes from my journals reflect the anguish and frustration that we experienced during this frightful period. Whenever life becomes too overwhelming, the only way that I know of to cope is to write it out. Somehow, writing helps me to externalize and absorb some of the pain from my inside. The following notes are excerpts from the various diaries that I wrote from July to October of that year.

Friday, July 22, 1988

11:30 a.m. R.S. McLaughlin School principal called and asked about Andi's medical problem. She told him that she has hyperglycemia and has to go to the hospital for shots and be tied down. I spoke to Andi about this and had a talk about lying, school, etc. (2:15 p.m.)

4:00 p.m. She went out. Said she was going to Debbie's and then to Terry's to dye his hair and she would call later.

5:00 p.m. Andi called and said she was going to the Kinsmen dance and asked if she could be home at 1:00 a.m. I told her no, to be in at her 12:30 curfew, and she said OK. We went out for dinner with some friends (Brian and Terri) and back to their new house for a visit. We left at 12:20 so we could be home when Andi got there. Got home—Bruce went to bed because he had to work in the morning, and I read the paper waiting for the kids to come in. At 1:00 a.m. when Andi wasn't home yet, I drove to the Kinsmen Hall looking for her on the way. No luck! Got back home at 1:20 and woke up Bruce. He went out looking—again no luck. Brad came home from work, and he and Bruce picked up Andrea's best friend Sarah to show them where Terry lived. We found out then that Terry did not live with his mom but on his own. A roomer in the building told us Andi went with two runaways (girls) and three black guys to drive into Scarborough and then to a hotel afterward.

2:15 a.m. Bruce brought Sarah and Brad home and was going back to the rooming house to wait for Andi's return. At the same time I called the police to report her missing. While I was on the phone, we heard an uproar outside. Andi had come in with another girl and guy. Bruce was so angry that he made the driver get out of the car. He took a swing at the guy, took away his car keys and drivers license, and told him that they were staying right there until the police showed up. He did this because the guy was trying to get away.

I stayed out to find out what had taken place that night. Meantime, in the house there was a lot of yelling, and finally Bruce left in his truck. I called the police and gave them his license number because we thought Bruce was going to see Terry, and Terry carries a knife.

After this I tried to talk to Andi but to no avail. She yelled things at me like:

- *I hate it here.*
- *I hate rules and curfews.*
- *I want a black baby to love and keep.*
- *I have no parents.*

- *I want to live on my own.*

At one point I slapped her and instantly regretted it. After trying to talk to her, I finally reached my limit and told her that if she really felt that strongly about it, to go get some clothes together and I would take her down to see a cop at the youth offenders and maybe they could do something with her. She agreed, and she and Brad and I went down to the police station at 3:15 a.m.

At the police station they told us there was no one in the youth bureau and to come back at 9:00 a.m. Andi refused to come back home with us. She became abusive, and the cop told us to let her walk the streets for the night. I just couldn't do this, and finally we reached a compromise. I took her to her friend Sarah's house, where she said she would stay until I picked her up at 9:00 a.m. to go back to the police station.

When we got back home Terry was at our house. I stayed in the car, and Brad spoke to him for about 10 minutes and then he left. At this point I didn't even want to know that Terry existed, let alone what they talked about.

Sarah's mom called at 5:15 a.m. She had just caught the girls sneaking back into the house. Sarah said Andi was running way, and she was trying to talk her into coming back

Saturday, July 23, 1988

8:45 a.m. I picked Andi up and went to the police station, where we talked to a constable from the youth bureau. After seeing him and because there was nothing that could be done before Monday, we tried to talk Andi into coming home until then. She adamantly refused, and we finally reached an agreement that she would find a place to stay and call me by 6 p.m. with a phone number so that we could contact her in case of an emergency. She called at 5:30 p.m. I talked to her for a minute and then passed the phone to Bruce. Andrea told him that she was going to have the lad who drove her home press charges of assault against Bruce and that if we tried to find her or tried to charge Terry, that she would leave the country. She gave us a phone number, and we asked her call again the

*next day (Sunday) to let us know that she was okay. When
we tried to call her, the number she gave us turned out to
be a disconnected line. We also noticed that there was money
missing, and Brad told us that she had tried to borrow $50
from him to help pay Terry's rent.*

Sunday, July 24, 1988

*11:30 a.m. Andrea called, not too concerned that the phone
number was not good. Told us she was staying with Tammy
(no last name), the girl who was in the car with her on Friday
night.*

*5:15 p.m. Andi called. Still wouldn't give us any info.
When we asked if she had eaten, she said no, she hadn't eaten
since Friday and didn't feel like it. She also said that she had
broken up with Terry because of the trouble she was in. I told
her that Carrie wanted to talk to her, and Andrea said Carrie
had gotten a hold of her, they were going to Elusions, and that
she might stay the night at Carrie's. I asked Carrie and Andi
to call me after they came home to let me know everything was
okay, but we waited up till 12:45 a.m. and no one called.*

Monday, July 25, 1988

*8:15 a.m. Andrea called, and, when she found out the time, she
hung up, saying would call again in an hour. In the meantime,
I spoke with Constable B at the youth bureau. He is writing
up a report that Andi is in need of protective custody and that
she is on a self-destructive course. He will submit this report
to CAS this afternoon. He had also spoken with the young lad
from Friday night. The result of the meeting was that the police
would not be pressing charges against Bruce, but the young lad
may very well do so. Something else to worry about! I called
CAS and made an appointment with Patti for 1:00 p.m.*

*9:40 a.m. Bruce called Andi's boss at the Dairy Queen,
and apparently Andrea was fired from her job because she
stole some money twice from the till. Andrea also told another
employee that she had stolen money and that she was 3 months
pregnant.*

9:50 a.m. I spoke with the principal of McLaughlin where Andrea is attending summer school. He said that Andrea was rude and abusive with her math teacher, and, when the principal talked to her, she became abusive with him. She was dismissed from math class on July 14. She had missed 3 days from school last week, and, when he questioned her, she had told him the story of the medical problems. He also said that Andrea could still come back and finish her science course.

Andrea called back and I told her about the appointment with CAS. She agreed to meet me at 12:00 so we could get something to eat before our appointment. When I said that Dad would be there too, she asked why, so Bruce said he would just meet us at the appointment in hopes that she would show up.

1:00 p.m. Bruce, Andi, and I met with Patti and discussed the problems that we have been having and tried to find a solution. It's 3:05 p.m. as I write this, and Andi is in with Patti right now in hopes that she can talk her into coming home for tonight until a solution can be found. We really are up against a solid brick_wall, and there is nothing more frustrating. The only reason that we can think of as to why Andi is acting this way is that she's pregnant, but she says that she's not. We have asked if we have the right to have a pregnancy test done, and Patti doesn't know but says she will find out.

"The tears I cry for you could fill and ocean, but you don't care how many tears I cry" is a line from an old song that's been going through my head for the past 24 hours. My emotions run the gamut from intense fear to anger, to emptiness to frustration, sadness and a sense of loss. I feel like my daughter has died and in her place has risen a monster. It's like the movies that you see on TV, where the person's body has been taken over by an evil thing. Either she's pregnant and running scared or someone has messed her head up so badly. I wonder if our Andi will ever return.

She says she hates her parents, and as far as she's concerned she has no family. What have we done to bring this about? Maybe if we knew, we could find a solution, but God knows we are almost at our limits. What is it that she really wants? It broke my heart to see her sitting there today. We agreed to meet early before the CAS meeting so that I could buy her something nutritious to eat. I came in from the back way and approached her from behind. What I saw was a person who looked defeated and dejected. There she sat, shoulders slumped, dressed in cold weather clothing on a hot summer's day, and puffing desperately on a cigarette. This, my baby, my big, grown-up 14-year-old who says she wants to be a mother when she's still a baby herself. What is she thinking? It scary to watch her trying to be tough. She wants nothing from us or anyone else. She wants to be left alone to live her own life on her own terms and in her own way. Can a 14–year-old know what she's asking of us? Does she have any idea of what the real world is like? I wonder! And worry and worry and worry. It's now 4:15 pm, and here the 3 of us sit waiting to find out—what?

Finally, we found out our options:

- *Talk her into coming home with us until something can be arranged. It could take weeks. (Andi says no way.)*
- *Charge her with theft and have her put into lockup.*
- *Let her go on staying wherever she pleases until something else can be arranged. Again, it could take weeks.*
- *Abandon her. She can walk the streets until she's picked up, and then we could get charged with abandonment.*
- *Try to have her made a ward of the court. Could take months, and no guarantee a judge would allow it.*
- *Pay for an apartment for her to stay in.*

What would you do?

I called the police station and spoke with Con. B to see if he could offer any advice or help. He asked the CAS worker to call him immediately, as he felt that Andrea needed protective custody. I am waiting for her (CAS worker) to come out so I can tell her this. Meanwhile, Andi sits here all nonchalant, and Bruce is like a caged lion. I can almost see his blood pressure rising. Me, I'm writing and putting myself (my mind) on hold so I can deal with this and keep my sanity. Finally Patti comes out and tells us the only thing she can offer is counseling. As she does not feel that Andrea is in any danger, they cannot take her in. In disgust and defeat, we leave.

When I got downstairs in the mall, I decided that I couldn't leave without talking to her once again. When she came down the stairs, I asked her to sit for a minute, don't talk, just listen, and then I told her we both loved her and that our door was open to her if she decided to return home, but it would be the conditions that were in place before.

I also told her to call us once in a while and that if she was pregnant, get something done about it, and if she wasn't, get to the doctor and get on some protection if she needed it. I told her that we would proceed with trying to get her in a group home and would keep her informed. I also told her to remember what it's like to have a family who loves you, a room of your own, to be able to take a couple of hours goofing off in the bathtub, and privacy when you needed it. She was almost in tears at this time, hugged me tight, and said she loved us. I left then. I'm writing this after coming home, and, as I write, my entire stomach is in revolt and I'm scared shitless that I've done the wrong thing. But I think this is something called tough love, where you let the child become responsible for their actions and their consequences. Please God, help me to be strong!

It's now 9 p.m. We came home discouraged and downtrodden. Bruce's instincts are telling him to seek out Terry and tear him apart limb by limb. His rage is all-consuming and is driving him toward a destructive path. I convinced him to paint Andi's bedroom ceiling for me, and I think that helped his frustration to have something else to focus on. We let our minds have a few hours Sabbath and then again discussed our worries. We have decided that we may have lost a battle today, but we sure as hell have not given up the fight. We've accepted today what we cannot change, but it does not mean we cannot change tomorrow. We still have hope and are encouraged that in the end our daughter will return to us.

It's 11:30 at night. It's pouring rain outside and thundering and lightening. Andi, where are you? Are you safe? Warm?

Dry? Or are you curled up on a park bench somewhere getting soaked by the rain pouring down? Did you have anything to eat tonight, or are you going hungry? I went up to bed, but every time I closed my eyes I saw you sitting in the mall waiting for me or else I relived my slapping you on Friday night. Needless to say, I am afraid to close my eyes. You may be very much alive, but you haunt me more than any ghost ever could. Please be safe, dry, and warm tonight.

Tuesday, July 26, 1988

Its 7:30 in the morning, and all three of us had no problem getting up. I dozed off finally on the chesterfield, and all night I could hear Bruce tossing and turning. He was also grinding his teeth so badly that I'm surprised he has any teeth left this morning. Even Brad is affected by all this. He appears to be concerned for us, and we in turn are pouring all of our love over him. God, I hope we don't smother him so bad that he wants to escape. I can understand now how this sometimes happens to families. Poor Brad has just acquired a new girlfriend and can't even take her out on a date this weekend because he is working 4–12 every night until Sunday. He has worked every day since last Thursday and going to summer school too. This is very hard on him.

I haven't had a chance to talk to Bruce this morning, so I'm not sure how he's feeling. I know when I looked in the mirror I barely recognize the person I'm becoming. I'm sure some of this pain must be showing on the outside. It has to because my insides are filled up and overflowing with it. My heart seems to be pumping and saying, "Andi, Andi, Andi, Andi." Does this ever go away and get replaced with acceptance of the way things are? We'll see. I called around trying to get info on group homes, and it will be after lunch before anyone gets back to me.

2:30 p.m. Talked to Constable B. He had a call from Terry, and as a result of the conversation he thinks it would be a good idea to report Andrea missing. He will send a cruiser over to our house to do a report.

3:50 p.m. Carna from Frontenac called about Andrea. She asked me to tell her what was going on, and, after about 20 minutes of conversation, the outcome was that it would be at least November before they could do an assessment and place her in a group home. I told her to go ahead with whatever needed to be done, and she said she would. In the meantime, if they could see her any sooner they would. Also, in the meantime, if Andi were charged, she would probably only get probation as a first offender. We could at that time press as a part of her probation that she stays away from anyone who is a known offender.

4:40 p.m. As of yet we have not heard a word from Andrea.

6:20 p.m. Found out from someone else that Andrea is living with Connie. (We don't know this person.)

Wednesday, July 27, 1988 (5 days gone)

4:00 p.m. Andrea came to the door with a female police officer to get her things. There was some confusion, as Andrea thought the officer was going to take her with her things to where she was going. The officer explained that they were not a taxi service. Another officer came, and, after some discussion, Andrea made some phone calls and said everything was okay, her friend was loaning her money for a cab. She left in the cab, and I followed. Sure enough, she went straight to Terry's place. I came home and called the cops. Guess what? They can't do a fucking thing about it and suggested I call Children's Aid. I feel like I have been slowly climbing out of the hole to hell all day, only to be pushed back to the bottom by Andrea. I want to find a hit person to put Terry on the moon in a million different pieces, the smaller the better. I'm almost to the point where I intensely hate my own daughter. How can one human being do to their parents what she's doing to us? Bruce is putting on a front that he almost doesn't care anymore but I know how sick he is inside. His fragile illusions of his daughter have been shattered. He is, however, very realistic, and he said deep inside he knows she's been lying to us all along. It's time to start thinking about letting go entirely and letting whatever happens, happen. I feel that way right now, but I know I will probably change my mind and start beating against the brick wall again.

5:20 p.m. I spoke to a worker at CAS, and, after explaining what was going on, she could offer no help but will check with her supervisor and call me back. She did call back about 15 minutes later and said there was nothing they could do because they had no info on Terry. But she said she would put a report on Patti's desk for tomorrow morning and perhaps between Patti and Constable B they could come up with a charge or some way to put Andrea in the care and custody of CAS.

5:45 p.m. I called Connie's and asked for Andrea. Connie said that she had been home all day and not heard anything from Andrea. This means Andrea's been lying to us because she said that she couldn't go there until after 6 p.m. I just asked Connie to have Andrea call when she heard from her.

Around 7:45 p.m. we still had not heard from Andrea but had to go out and run some errands. When we got back around 9:15, Andrea had left a message for us to call her at Connie's. Bruce called and spoke to her for about 15 minutes. He said she was hostile at first but got a little friendlier after a few minutes. She outright refused to admit that she had been to Terry's and flatly denied that she went there at all today. She agreed to meet Bruce for lunch tomorrow and told her he could pick her up at an intersection by Terry's place because she would there in the morning.

Thursday, July 28, 1988

8:15 a.m. Constable B called and asked how things were going. After catching him up, he checked with another officer who had checked on Andrea's whereabouts last night. That officer reported that she was at Connie's, where she was supposed to be. He is also going to talk to CAS and get back to us.

Friday, July 29, 1988

I called CAS and the police, but so far nothing is happening. Andrea called around 6:00 p.m. to ask when Grandma was coming up and said she would call before coming over to see her.

Saturday, July 30, 1988
No calls from anyone, including Andrea.

Sunday, July 31, 1988
We waited as long as we could, and by 6:00 p.m. when we hadn't heard from Andrea, we starting phoning around looking for her. There was no answer at Terry's, and Connie says she hasn't talked to her since Thursday but said that she was expecting her to come back sometime tonight. I asked her to have Andrea call because we were worried about her. When we still hadn't heard anything by 10:15 p.m. I called Connie. Nothing ... and still no answer at Terry's.

Well Andrea, you called on Friday to ask about Grandma, and in the end said, "Okay, I'll call tomorrow or Sunday. It's now 10:30 on Sunday night, and we're starting to get frantic all over again. We went out with Grandma for a couple of hours today, but you know enough to leave a message with the answering service and you haven't even given us that courtesy. No one answers the phone at Terry's (I can barely write his name for the hatred that rises when I think of him), and we think you went into Toronto to Caribana this weekend. Did you, or is this maniac a pimp who's putting you out on the streets? If he is, his life is not worth shit, and I will gladly plunge the knife deeply into him myself without giving a second thought. I find it hard to believe that any human being can have this much hatred for another human being, but it has happened and it is very real! Tomorrow morning, if I have not heard from you, I will call the police and report you missing. I only hope that something terrible hasn't happened in the meantime. Please, please, see this animal for what he is and come back where you belong with your family that loves you, no strings attached. We only want you to be safe, happy, and healthy. I pray to hear from you soon. Love Mom, Dad, and Brad.

Monday, August 1, 1988

It's early in the morning, before eight o'clock, and I'm finally glad the long night is over. They say that when people drink the truth comes out. If this is true, then Bruce blames me for the situation we're in. He said (jokingly) that I beat (slapped) Andrea and that's why she wanted to go to the police station that night. He also stated that when he left that night Andrea was at home, so it had to be something I did. I've been thinking about that all night, and probably what he says is true. I realized that I've had these same thoughts in the back of my mind all along, and, when I heard them aloud, they hit me with full force. When Bruce said that last night, a part of me (either the sensitive or childish side) curled into a knot so tight that I don't know if it can be untied. I'll have to gently try to gradually untie it. In the meantime, I feel like part of me is missing. Maybe all this mess is my fault! I'm not surprised. I'm always screwing something up, even if it's not intentional. So I'll admit blame here and now, kick myself in the ass, get up, and keep on trying to make things right again. Maybe it can be done, and maybe it can't. Time will tell, and I hope we have lots of time.

10:35 a.m. Finally got an answer at Terry's place. Andrea answered the phone. I got her out of bed and just talked to her long enough to make sure she was okay and then told her to call me back when she was awake. She said that she had tried to call us over the weekend but either the line was busy or there was no answer.

She called back about an hour later and said she wanted to visit Grandma. I invited her for supper, and she said yes without hesitation. Then around 4:30 she called and said she had just finished a sub, so she wasn't hungry and would come by after supper. She came over around 7:30 and stayed about 45 minutes and left, taking her bike with her. She said she was starting a new job at Rave tomorrow morning at 10:00 a.m. The only other things she talked about was all the fighting among her friends, how another friend had committed suicide on Friday night, and how another girl wanted to pound her head in because Andrea told her that she wouldn't miss her if she succeeded during one of her many attempts. Andrea also told us that Terry was in Toronto and that he was going back to Jamaica for 2 weeks because his brother had been killed in a car accident. She said that she would be staying at his place in the meantime and that the rent was paid until September 1st. When questioned if she ever took her things to Connie's, she was evasive and said her stuff was all over the place.

Tuesday, August 2, 1988
No calls—no news.

Wednesday, August 3, 1988
Andrea called and spoke to Bruce for about 5 minutes.

Thursday, August 4, 1988
No calls—no news.

Friday, August 5, 1988
No calls—no news.

Saturday, August 6, 1988
I called Andrea around 10:30 a.m. because we hadn't heard from her, and we had to go to a wedding in the afternoon. Terry answered the phone (so Andrea lied about him going away) and then put Andrea on. I told her I was just making sure that she was okay, and she said she had no news. Later, between the wedding and reception, we went down to Tom and Helen's (my sister). Helen's daughters stepped in to see if they could help in any way. Tracy called Andrea to ask her out for supper, and Andrea accepted. Tammy decided to go along too. They said they would call me on Sunday and let me know how they made out. Later we were talking to a cousin of Bruce's who went to school with Andrea. She said that she had run into Andrea and that she thought Andrea had changed a lot.

Sunday, August 7, 1988

Tammy and Tracy talked to Andrea but to no avail. Terry was also there, and Tracy lost her cool because Terry hovered around Andrea, fixing her clothes, hair, etc. They talked to her and suggested that Andrea go to Helen's or elsewhere for a week with no contact from us or Terry. Andrea refused and said she could do her thinking where she was.

Monday, August 8, 1988

Andrea called and just said she was okay.

Tuesday, August 9, 1988

No calls—no news.

Wednesday, August 10, 1988

No news from Andrea. CAS called and will contact Andrea about counseling. Patti will call back next week to let me know if she had any luck.

Thursday, August 11, 1988

Mona and Richard came down with the kids. Mona and I took Grandma home to Belleville and then went to visit Lois and Karl. No news at all from Andrea.

Friday, August 12, 1988

Andrea called and agreed to meet us at Tom and Helen's for supper and a swim. She had spent Thursday night at her friend Crystal's house. She was at Tom and Helen's when Bruce and I got there around 5:30 and stayed till about 7. Then she said she had to go because she was going to a wedding shower.

Saturday, August 13, 2007

Betty and Ken came up from Belleville for a visit. Mona, Richard, Bruce, and I all went down to see them at Tom and Helen's. Betty called Andrea, and she agreed to come over for a visit. Bruce and Richard took all the kids to the circus, and Betty and Tom sat down with Andrea and had a talk with her about AIDS, birth control, etc. Then Betty decided she wanted to meet Terry. I dropped Betty and Andrea off and then took off for about 15 minutes. When I came back, I had to wait about another 15 minutes. Andrea came out and asked me to get Betty out of there because she was embarrassing her. I got Betty out, and we went back to Tom and Helen's. There was a big discussion, and Betty thought Terry seemed to be okay but did not like Terry's friend who was there. She also said she looked in the fridge, and the only thing there was a package of Lipton soup and some gross-looking meat.

Friday, August 26, 2008

Nothing new has happened until today. Andrea has called every day or so just for a minute—long enough to let us know she's okay. She mentioned coming home a couple of times, but, when I tried to pin her down about it, she became evasive and gave non-committal answers like, "I don't know. When I'm ready."

She called this morning about 11:30, and Bruce was here. He said he didn't want to talk to her and told me to tell her that if she's planning on coming home it had better be soon or she could forget it. It would be too late. She was either part of the family or she's not, and she'd better make a decision soon. Andi said okay and that she had to go. It was a very short conversation.

Bruce hasn't been sleeping well all week. He's been worrying about Andrea, and I guess he's reached his limit. We discussed his ultimatum and wondered if I should tell her not to call again until she was ready to come home. We decided against that because we still wanted to keep the doors of communication open. We also discussed the rules when she did decide to come home, including:

- *There would still be curfew.*
- *She would have to keep her room clean and her laundry done.*
- *She would have to go to counseling.*

- *She would have to have a complete physical with a D&A evaluation if required.*

We also discussed some of the tough love tactics and finally decided that we were ready and waiting for Andrea to make up her mind. Fortunately, we didn't have long to wait.

Around 9:45 p.m. Tracy called and said she had just had a very strange phone call from Andrea and Terry. She said Andrea sounded like she had been crying, and Terry wanted to talk to her to set the record straight that he was really a nice guy and not the rotten person that everyone was making him out to be. Tracy offered to pick Andrea up, but she said no. I no sooner hung up the phone from Tracy when it rang again. It was Terry, and he asked to speak to "my husband." He talked to Bruce for about 10 minutes, and, during the course of the discussion, he said Andrea was drinking and smoking dope and hadn't paid a cent since she moved in. He said he had told her to go home numerous times. Bruce said it sounded like he was getting sick of her and looking for a way to get her out. He ended the conversation, and about 15 minutes later I called back to make sure she was okay. Terry said she had gone out with Crystal and her mom. I told him to have Andrea call me when she came back. In the meantime, Crystal showed up at our door and said she'd promised Andrea she would talk to us about setting up a meeting maybe Sunday and an appointment at CAS for Monday so she could start counseling. We told Crystal that was okay with us but that there were other considerations and that Andrea was going to have to make a true effort to want to straighten herself out— no more lying, stealing, etc.

Crystal said there were a lot of things she wanted to tell us but had promised Andrea she wouldn't. I asked her to tell us and that we would keep it confidential. These are some of the things that she told us:

- *Terry beats Andrea. He has a stick that he uses, or he kicks her or slaps her. Her arms and legs are covered with bruises, and tonight he hit her in the head with a can opener and she was bleeding. When Crystal wanted to call the police, Andrea wouldn't let her. She also has a bruise on her face. Apparently, these things have been happening all along.*

- *There had been no food in the house for weeks. Andrea and Terry went to a food bank today for food. Crystal has been bringing Andrea food from her house.*

- *Terry plays mind games with Andrea all the time (e.g., telling her she could go somewhere and then when she was ready, telling her she couldn't go; telling her to do something and when she takes a step to do it, telling her to stop). Crystal also said that she stops exactly where she is and doesn't move until he says it's okay. When she threatens to call the police, he picks up the phone and dials the number, knowing that she won't go through with it.*

- *Terry tells her friends not to bug him too much or he'll take it out on her when they leave.*

- *Terry orders pizza and then won't let her have any.*

- *-Terry has no visible means of support. He either sells drugs, collects welfare, or lives off his mom and brother. He says his brother brings drugs from Toronto for him to sell.*

- *Andrea does not have any job right now.*

- *-Andrea says she is pregnant, but Crystal doesn't think she is.*

In the meantime, Andrea called back, and we set up a meeting for Sunday at 3 p.m. at the lake to discuss her coming home on Monday. After hearing all of this, I was really upset, and we decided that if Andrea wanted out, come hell or high water, we would get her out. We made a few phone calls to get backup, and then had Crystal call Andrea. Crystal told her if she wanted out that we would come and get her and her things out of there now. Andrea said no, that it was the weekend, and that she would wait until Monday. I then gave Crystal a ride home, as it was after midnight. Needless to say, neither Bruce not I slept at all that night.

Saturday, August 27, 1988

Today is a waiting day. It seems like forever until Sunday!

Sunday, August 28, 1988

As it was raining on Sunday morning, we called Andrea and told her if it was still raining at three o'clock, we would pick her up at Terry's. If not, we would meet as planned at the lake. At 2:45 it was cloudy but fairly warm, so we went to the lake and Andrea was already there waiting. The first thing she wanted was a hug. Then we walked along the boardwalk and out on to the pier and discussed a number of things. Andrea said she missed us, and we agreed upon the following:

- *She is to have a complete checkup.*
- *Curfew is 9:30 through the week and 1:00 a.m. on weekends.*
- *She has to keep her room clean and laundry done.*
- *No smoking in the house.*
- *No phone calls after 10 p.m.*

We discussed a number of other things, and Andrea told us that she was looking for a job, she was going to try to do better in school, and she didn't expect us to buy her new clothes to go back to school.

We told her that any of her friends are welcome in the house except Terry and that we do not expect her to leave the house in the morning and to spend her day hanging around his apartment. We were all going to try to do our best to communicate and work things out. If Andrea screwed up through the week, she would be grounded 2 weeknights. If on the weekends, she would be grounded the following weekend. She was agreeable to this, and we set up a time to pick her and all of her stuff up to come home. We would be picking her up around 1 p.m. on Monday.

We also talked to her and Brad separately about their attitude toward each other. They agreed that if they didn't have anything positive to say, they wouldn't say anything. (I'll believe that when I see it!)

Monday, August 29, 1988

Andrea came home with all her stuff and spent the afternoon unpacking and getting organized. I'm optimistic that everything will be okay eventually, but we shall see.

Thursday, September 1, 1988

Well it's been 4 days. I don't know if they've been good or bad. It's like Andrea never left. It seems to me that she is still trying to manipulate me and thumbing her nose at me at the same time. Little does she know that I'm on to her, and, instead of impressing me, she is making me harden my heart even more.

She said she had to do laundry right away, but tonight I had to practically force her to do it. On Wednesday I had to do some errands and then was going to the shopping center. I asked her if she wanted to come with me, and I would take her out for lunch. While I was running errands, she was trying to talk me into letting her drive the car and trying to impress me with these stories of how everyone else's mom was so impressed with her. She wanted to go to Red Lobster for lunch and ordered popcorn shrimp. When they came, she said she didn't even like shrimp and only ate 2 of them with her fries. She also tried to talk me into spending money on her for clothes shopping. When she talked about coming home, we told her she would have to stay with a friend from Thursday to Sunday because we already had plans and a hotel booked in Ottawa to get away from everything for a few days. She agreed and said she could stay with Sarah. On Wednesday night at seven o'clock, she called and said that she had nowhere to stay and neither did Sarah because her parents were going away too. She asked if she and Sarah could go to Ottawa with us. I was furious! We debated and tried other avenues, and finally it was either cancel or take them with us. We decided to take them with us.

On Thursday morning I gave Andrea $20.00 plus bus fare to get her hair cut. She came back, and I really have my doubts as to whether she went to a hairdresser. Her hair is about 2" shorter in the front but hasn't been touched on the sides or *back. She said it cost $16.00 and that she used the other 4 bucks for lunch. (If she paid for the haircut, it couldn't have been more than $5.00 because it was only cut a bit in the front—no wash/dry or anything.) Anyway, I feel like she is doing more and more to alienate me. She gets on the phone with Terry and then talks ridiculously about nothing. We'll see how the weekend goes, but I will take no shit from her!*

Sunday: Andrea did everything she could to ruin our weekend, from ordering food and then not eating it to ordering movies at the hotel and generally grumbling about everything that we suggested to do. Rotten weekend\bad lunch\haircut?

Monday, September 12, 1988
Talked to Dianna at CAS about problems still having. She will enquire about getting Andi in for counseling.

September 19, 1988
I had eight teeth extracted today. (I have always been plagued with problems with my teeth and have finally decided that it's time for dentures—this is the first step in getting that accomplished.)

September 20, 1988
Dr. Roy got results from Andrea's test. Andrea's pregnancy test was positive. Because Andrea says this is impossible, Dr. Roy is redoing all tests and will get back to us. Does this nightmare ever end? The only bit of light I can see is that Frontenac has set up an appt. for Nov 10.

September 21, 1988
I called the school. Andrea has been off sick one day and has skipped 3 others—all within the first 12 days of the new school year.

September 22, 1988
Andrea left her books behind, so I called school and guess what—Andrea didn't show up there today. Bruce and I have

done so much talking and worrying about making the right decisions. We finally gave Andrea a choice about her pregnancy. She can have an abortion and start over, or if she decides to continue with the pregnancy she has to get out and is no longer a part of our family. She is to think about it and give us an answer on Sunday. (We are so exhausted by all this and have been informed by the police that Terry now has 3 girls pregnant here in Oshawa and is looking for a way to stay in Canada.) If Andrea has this child, he could become a permanent part of her as well as our future. I would never have believed it possible that I could be a violent person, but I hate this man with every cell of my being. I have even thought about how to go about having him killed. As far as I am concerned, he has hurt my child beyond anything that I can fathom. Right now I am so filled with hatred for him that I could stand in front of him, put a knife into his gut, turn it slowly, and watch him die. God help us all!

Friday, September 23, 1988

Brad had his first car accident today. It was only a fender bender, but he was really upset. Also, one of our employees was crossing the railway tracks and a train without lights or warning hit him. He is okay, but our dump truck was totaled.

Sunday, September 25, 1988

Andrea has decided that she will go through with the abortion. We told her that we thought she was doing the right thing, but I don't think she truly believes us. Maybe in the future.

Monday, September 26, 1988

We found out that Terry was being in held in Whitby Jail by immigration and just got out today at 11:30. We think Andrea went to see him tonight, and we're afraid he's going to try to talk her into having this baby so she can be his ticket to stay in Canada. God help us!

Tuesday, September 28, 1988

All was quiet at home until about 6:45 p.m. That's when the police came the door looking for Brad. Apparently, he got into a fight with a kid on a bike who had gotten too close to his car. That's all I know for now, and Bruce is out at a Landscape Ontario meeting right now.

Wednesday, September 29, 1988

Sarah's mom called and wanted to know if Andrea was at school yesterday. I called the school, and apparently she hasn't been there since September 23!

The next part of this story is not written anywhere because up to now it has been too painful. I still feel guilty and ashamed of the choice that we forced Andrea, a fourteen-year-old, to make. Even though we gave her a choice, was it really a choice? Did we have the right to do that to her? At the time, it was the only solution we could see. We were too worn out from the months and years of trials and tribulations between her and Brad to take on the added responsibility of another child, and, being adopted myself, even though I had a wonderful family, it was a very emotionally painful path. We also felt that Andrea was too smart to end up on welfare with a baby at fourteen years old. So we did what we thought was best at the time.

We arranged for Andrea and me to fly to Detroit to an abortion clinic that was recommended by a local pro-choice group. We flew out of Oshawa Airport very early in the morning and took a cab straight to the clinic. As the clinic had advised us to stay overnight in case there were any complications, we had made arrangements to stay in a motel close by. A few hours after arriving in Detroit, the abortion was complete, and we were in a motel room for the night. The doctor at the clinic had come out to see me in the waiting room following the procedure. He told me that the baby had been a boy and then he asked some questions about the father's ethnic background. He then went over the aftercare that Andrea would require and shortly afterward released her and allowed us to leave.

Andrea was not overly communicative, and I guess I wasn't up to saying too much either. We took a cab to the motel, and she turned the television on and then crawled into bed and slept off and on until the next morning when it was time to leave. I couldn't have slept a wink. I just sat in the chair or lay on the bed and watched her all night long. My heart felt as though it was broken into a million pieces, and I was filled with the guiltiest and most horrible feeling of dread in the world.

We returned home the next day without any discussion about what had happened. I don't know if it was guilt or shame or whether it was just something we didn't even know how to talk about, but the whole subject was swept under the rug as though it had never happened. Within the next few weeks, Andrea appeared to return to her normal self. The pregnancy was not spoken of again for many years. Even though Andrea still has never shared her feelings other than to say it was the best solution, I'm sure she did her own grieving in her own way. It has always been in the back of my mind, and I have kept track of how old that child would have been. Only three years later I began to believe that because of this choice I was being punished and had to pay for circumstances that I had set in motion.

Andrea gradually began to conform eventually and straightened up her act somewhat, thank goodness. Terry was eventually deported back to Jamaica. I have never set eyes on him since, and Andrea has never spoken of him again.

Chapter 23
I Don't Have Time for a Brain Tumor—We're Moving Again!

They say when it rains it pours, and that seems to be an adequate description in our case. On top of all the troubles going on with Brad and Andrea, I had ongoing problems with migraine headaches and had been seeing doctor after doctor and trying every available medication. My energy levels were almost nonexistent. As a last resort, our family doctor sent me to a neurologist, who did a number of tests. He didn't determine the cause of the headaches, but he did discover something else. I had a tumor in the right temporal lobe. Another series of testing would determine whether it was malignant. If it was a meningioma as he suspected, surgery would be elective; however, if it was malignant, I would have to undergo surgery as soon as it could be arranged.

I remember dreading having to pass this information along to Bruce. I went home telling myself that it was no big deal and not to look for trouble where there might not be any. I was standing in front of the kitchen sink making supper when he came in. I tried acting normal, but, as soon as he started talking, I turned around to face him and started crying. The funny thing was that my biggest worry was that they would have to shave my head! We talked about it and could do nothing but wait for the results. In the meantime, of course I thought about it nonstop and made the decision that if it was elective surgery, then I elected to not have it. To hell with what the doctor had to say! I would make the decision, not someone else.

The good news was that it was a benign tumor, and, when I told the doctor how I felt, he was agreeable to waiting as long as I was willing to be monitored. Finally, a doctor I could work with! For the next few years, I went every six months and then every year for a while.

When our life was turned upside down in 1990, I completely forgot about the tumor until 2005.

Life over those next few years was relatively quiet. We had our usual difficulties, and the business continued to struggle along. We were always cash poor but knew that we were equity strong. There were times that Bruce and I didn't get a paycheck and were sometimes slow getting the bills paid, but we always made sure our employees were paid. We had a nice home in a good neighborhood and a large shop, out of which we ran the business. One day, when Bruce was at the shop doing some welding, something went awry, and there was a huge fire. We lost a truck, quite a lot of equipment, and the use of the shop.

It is said that when one door closes, another opens, and that's what happened. A guy who did our excavating work had an acre of land closer to the city, and it had a house and a shop on it. He and his wife wanted to move back to the East Coast and semiretire, and he provided us with the solution that we badly needed. He offered to sell us his place and, with a down payment, he would hold the mortgage. As Bruce's dad had passed away not long before this time, there was a small inheritance, and Bruce talked his brother into using all of the money for the down payment on the property. We moved our business to this new location and rented the house out for a few years. Then we gradually realized that it would be more beneficial to buy his brother Glen out, sell our house, and build a new house on this property. That way we could have our home and business all in one place. We moved ahead with those plans, but, by the time we got our place sold and were ready to move, the real estate market had taken a dive. So we felt that it would be more economical to renovate the existing house instead of tearing it down and rebuilding.

We spent many hours designing a house that would work for us with two teenagers, as well as later on when we would be empty nesters. I even made sure all the doorways would accommodate a wheelchair so I wouldn't have to move again.

Brian, who had been a friend of ours since he was fourteen, rose to the challenge of being our general contractor and took six months off work to help us with the renovations. Brian had started working for us part-time in high school and then worked full-time for a few years. He had eventually gone to work at General Motors and had started up his own landscaping business on the side. From the moment he had come into our lives, there was something about him that couldn't really be defined, but he was a best friend to both Bruce and me. He was like the younger brother who was always around when you needed him. He was funny and smart and if a day went by without him stopping in at our house, we would wonder what was wrong. He was like a soul mate to both of us, and he and I talked for hours about things that I have never even talked to Bruce about. I don't think there was a thing about each other that we didn't know. He was probably the same with Bruce, but I never asked because I do believe that every person has the right to keep his own secrets if he needs to.

With the enormous task of renovating, we set a start date of May 1, 1990. When we had moved out of our other house, we put everything in storage except for our beds, one dresser each, an old couch and chair, and a television. I also moved our office desk into the new place, and I continued to run the office during the renovations. Let me tell you that living in a house while you are doing extensive renovations is a challenge that most people, including me, will only take on once.

As we progressed, my office shifted from room to room. We were in complete chaos from May until about mid-October that year. For about three of those months, I did not have a kitchen and was washing dishes in the bathtub. We ate fast food constantly, and it seemed as though we would get up early in the morning and stop to go to bed, only to get up and do it all over again. There was plaster dust everywhere. Our kitchen table was our old patio set, and I'm sure that more often than not we were consuming dust with our dinner. The good news was that we had very little rain that summer, and, when we did get rain, it would come in the night and be gone by morning. Because of this, we didn't lose any precious time to the weather. The other amazing thing was that Brian and I had only one disagreement during the whole process. He was practically living with us but was so easy to deal with that we all got along pretty well. He was also pretty goofy, and, whenever anything would get too serious, he would pull a stunt and have us all in gales of laughter. He and Bruce pulled practical jokes on almost every person that worked on the house, and, although most of them laughed it off, I'm sure a few of them thought we were more than a little weird.

One of the jokes that they pulled was on a poor fellow from

Newfoundland who was building a retaining wall and doing some odd jobs for us. If you know anything about "Newfies," you know that they have a wonderful and very charming brogue, and, when they get excited, their accent gets so thick that you can hardly understand them. Well, Brian had cleaned out a house that had been foreclosed on by a bank, and the house had belonged to a doctor. Left in the house was a very real-looking skull that Brian decided not to dispose of. One day when the Newfie was digging a trench and had left for lunch, Bruce and Brian got the big idea that they would plant this skull ahead of where he was digging. It was easily accomplished because the whole area had been excavated recently. They planted the skull and then went back to their respective work to wait. About an hour after the guy returned, they heard one hell of screech, and this poor guy came running up the knoll as white as a sheet, barely coherent and thinking that he had just uncovered a buried body. Bruce and Brian, being the good actors that they were, appeared concerned and amazed. I think they tried to talk the poor guy into digging further in case there was a body to go with the head, but he would have none of it. After they speculated about a murder and all kinds of other scenarios, they finally let the poor guy off the hook by telling him what they had done. The Newfie thought it was pretty funny once he knew that it was a joke, but I'm sure it was a moment he would never forget.

That was one of the more memorable of the practical jokes, but they were happening all the time. When I look back at that summer, I forget all of the hard work and the inconvenience and remember instead the good times and the fun that we had. One of those times, the joke was on us. Our house was on a busy, main road, and part of the renovation entailed removing the stone on the front of the house. Until the additions were finished, all we had for outside walls were two-by-sixes covered in plastic. One night, while we were sleeping, it got quite windy, and the plastic blew off. It also blew our bedroom door open, and, when we woke up in the morning, there we were, on display for everyone going by to see. I don't know if anyone actually noticed, but talk about feeling exposed!

One of the not so good times happened in January, just after we had moved into the house and begun renovating. Brad was eighteen years old and still hated school. I think he missed a lot of time there, but was very responsible at work and in other ways. He had a girlfriend, and I guess he thought his time with her and his friends were more important than school. He began staying out late on school nights, which became a real bone of contention for Bruce and me. We questioned our right to tell him what to do because, at eighteen years old, he was considered an adult. But things got out of hand one school night when he didn't come in until after 2 AM. Then he didn't want to get up to go to classes the next day. Consequently, we got into one hell of a fight with him, and he chose to leave home.

He was really angry when he left, and we did not hear from him for about three days. Finally, he called and told us that he was staying with a friend's brother and would be rooming there for a while. He didn't tell us, but he had quit school and decided to work instead. He and Bruce did not talk for a while longer, but eventually they made up. Brad even started working for Bruce part-time when he wasn't at his other job. We had so many other things on our plate during this time and Brad seemed to be doing okay, so we just let things be. We figured that he may want to move back after the house was finished, but he was an adult now and it was much different from when Andrea had left us.

Brad eventually began working in the family business full-time, and, as he seemed to be really maturing, Bruce began to seriously reconsider his dream of Brad taking over the family business one day. It was normal for Brad to come to dinner a couple of nights a week, and lots of times I sent care packages home with him to make sure that he ate. He was going out with Wendy, who we really liked because she was a good influence on him. She was away at university studying to become a teacher and only managed to come home at holidays. When Wendy had left for school in September, there wasn't much to see at our house. It was still pretty much torn apart. By Thanksgiving, when she came home, Brad brought her up to see the progress. Later, he told me that they had joked about how, in a few years, they could build Bruce and me a cabin out back and he and Wendy could move into the house, run the business, and raise the sixteen kids that Brad wanted. I guess that meant that they were looking at a lifetime together, and that made me feel pretty good about his future.

In the meantime, we worked our asses off getting the three

additions put on, moving walls, putting in new bathrooms, and all of the numerous things required to get the house the way we wanted. Bruce increased his garages from a double to a three car garage and of course other changes were constantly being made. By early October, we finally had the majority of the work done, and it was beginning to look like a real house again. The new drywall was finished, and basically all that was left was to prime and paint all of the walls and window frames. A couple of friends came to help me and we got the majority of it done so that the carpet and flooring could be installed.

What a wonderful Thanksgiving we had that year. The house was 99 percent complete, and all of my things were back. It was like an early Christmas as I opened each box to reveal things that I had almost forgotten about. We had a real home again, and all that we needed was to finish painting the trim and start living again. Life was good!

Following that Thanksgiving weekend, I was busy with some volunteer work. From the time that Brad had started in Beavers (Boy Scouts), I had volunteered as a leader and gradually worked my way up to the service team, which monitored different groups to ensure everything was going smoothly. I took a lot of training and then started doing provincial training for groups. Camp Samac, a local scouting area, became my second home, and I spent as much time there as I did at home sometimes. I had recently gotten another promotion with scouting and was in charge of a three-part "Part II Wood Badge" course. It included Beavers, Cubs, and Scouts and was being run for the first time in our district. All together, there were about eighty participants, and it was my job to oversee the whole thing. Because it was my first time in this capacity, I was to have a mentor. Unfortunately, he wasn't available when the time came, but I mustered through the best I could. The three weekends went quite well on the surface but underneath all of those old feelings of inadequacy and not being good enough kicked into high gear and by the end of the course I personally felt that I had met my level of incompetence, even though my higher-ups insisted that I had done a great job. Maybe, my gut was trying to tell me that something was not quite right, and I just wasn't listening properly.

With all the hard work on the house behind us and the scouting training completed, Bruce and I felt that we had earned a well-deserved holiday. We booked a trip for Antigua in November to coincide with our twentieth anniversary. I finished my three-weekend scouting course on Sunday around two in the afternoon, and we drove straight to a hotel by the airport because we were leaving very early Monday morning. I was totally exhausted, but the trip was good. For some reason, I had an underlying feeling of impending doom deep inside me. In part, I think it had to do with my feeling of inadequacy with the course I had just finished, and I was also thoroughly convinced that Bruce had suggested we go there so that he could ask me for a divorce. Don't ask me why. That was the overriding thought that I had the whole time we were away. He had never given me any reason to doubt that he loved me, but the uneasy feeling persisted. Finally, before we came home, I asked him about it. Of course, he said no most emphatically, but I was still convinced something was terribly wrong.

While we were in Antigua, we bought gifts to bring back to the kids. We got Brad a diver's watch. He would constantly forget to take his watch off when he had a bath or shower, so we figured this was a good solution for him. I can't remember what we brought Andrea back, but the watch was to play a significant role in Bruce's life for a long time.

Chapter 24
Our World Falls Apart

We were back from our holiday at the end of November and started thinking about our first Christmas in our new house. Andrea and Brad had both settled down tremendously over the past few years, and we were beginning to think that the worst years were behind us. We had invited Grandma Brunette up for Christmas, as she enjoyed coming to visit. She came around December 15, and we went Christmas shopping, did some baking, and in general enjoyed the Christmas season. We had our company Christmas dinner booked for December 19, and the only thing left to do was for me to have a final, wrap-up meeting on the scouting course I had recently finished. The meeting was booked at my house for December 18. Grandma and I shopped most of the day, and then Helen and Tammy came up for a visit and kept Grandma occupied while I was in my meeting.

Just after the meeting started, Brad called to tell me that Wendy would be home and he would be bringing her to the company Christmas dinner the next night. He was in a good mood and was joking around and asking me what I had bought him for Christmas, but I cut the call short, telling him that I was in a meeting and would talk to him tomorrow. I finished my meeting, and, when I came back out in the kitchen, Grandma and the girls had finished off a bottle of wine. Everyone was in high spirits. Bruce came in from shopping for Brad and Andrea and had dropped everything in the hallway for me to wrap and put under the tree. Even though I have always done most of the Christmas shopping, Bruce has always made a point of going out to get something special for the kids just from him. This year, because Brad would be working out in the snow and freezing cold, Bruce had stocked up on new jeans, sweaters, gloves, socks, a hat and scarf, and all kinds of things to make sure he would be warm.

We spent the rest of the evening visiting and when I went to bed that night, I had one of those rare moments when everything feels exactly right in the world. I've only had this feeling a few times before, and it's a pretty nice feeling. I used to get it when the kids would come in after work or being out and they would touch my foot just to let me know they were home safe. Once they did that, I would roll over and fall into a proper sleep, knowing everything was okay.

At ten to six the next morning, the doorbell rang. I put my housecoat on and went to the door, where a police officer was standing. He asked to speak to Bruce, and I didn't think anything of it because in the past police officers had come to the door early in the morning to deliver summonses for some of our employees. Nonetheless, when he asked for Bruce and then enquired if there was someplace private that he could talk to him, I crept closer and listened in.

He asked Bruce if we had a son named Brad. When Bruce said yes, the officer told him that there had been a fatal car accident on the 401 near Deseronto, just east of Belleville. At these words, I flew into the office to stand by Bruce. The officer said some other things, but I did not hear them. My mind was shut off and racing at the same time. I told him there must be some mistake because Brad was in Oshawa. Someone must have stolen his ID and the truck; and that it must be somebody else. Bruce tried to tell me that it was no mistake, but I refused to believe it. The police needed someone to ID the body at Belleville Hospital, and I immediately thought of calling my sister Betty who lived in Belleville. I figured that she would go over; see that it was not Brad, and this charade would be over. In the end it was Betty's husband, Ken, and my nephew Scott who went. They called back to confirm that it really was Brad. My world just shut off. I refused to call anyone until we knew for sure and then we had to make some phone calls—the type of calls that I hope I never have to make again.

Within an hour, our house was filled with family and friends, all wanting to help in whatever way they could. Brian Zam, who could have been our friend Brian's twin and did all of our excavating for us, was at the door minutes after it was announced on the news and told us that he would go to the shop, tell our employees and take care of everything there for us for as long as it would take.

That day is still very surreal. The coroner in Belleville would not release Brad's body until he had performed an autopsy, which would take a couple of days. In the meantime, there were things to be taken care of. Bruce came in to me and told me that he had to go to the accident site. He didn't know why, he just needed to go. We talked about it, and I agreed that, while he did that, I would go to the funeral home and make arrangements and pick out a cemetery plot. Brian and Ken went with Bruce to the accident site while my brothers-in-law, Tom and Glen, took me to do what I had to do. Everyone that we dealt with at the funeral home and cemetery were very understanding and extremely helpful. We made all the arrangements and then came back home. I was insistent that the funeral home do everything that they could so that we could have an open casket. I could not even fathom not being able to see Brad again.

When we got back home, I had to find Brad's suit and iron a white shirt for him. I did this for a long time, not wanting to stop because it meant taking the next step in this nightmare. I went into the Christmas shopping bags that Bruce had brought home the night before to get some warm socks. I don't know why, but it was of utmost importance that Brad would not have cold feet. At one point, I was walking across the hall between the living room and our bedroom and in my head I was screaming, "Why me, Lord?" and just like a slap up the side of the head I heard, "Why not you?" At that moment, I got a wakeup call, and I truly realized that none of us are exempt from life's pain.

Someone had called our family doctor, and he sent over a prescription for Bruce and me. I don't know what it was, but it was horrible. I took it once, and, every time I would start to think about what had happened, my mind would go blank. After that, I only pretended to take them and would get rid of them when no one was looking. I figured that I needed a clear head to face whatever was coming and to look after Bruce and Andrea.

Bruce was in worse shape than I was, only in a different way I think. He grasped the reality immediately, while I either went into denial or idealized with my own wishes and desires. While I knew what was happening was real, I put myself on hold until everything was done. When Bruce came back that first day from the accident site, he said it felt like Brad's soul was lost and wandering around, bewildered by what was going on. He was really glad that he went, because he felt that he brought that part of Brad back with him.

After what seemed like forever, we finally got Brad's body back for the wake. The coroner had determined that he had died instantly from severe head injuries. He had not been wearing his seat belt and almost every bone in his body had been broken. The police had determined that he had either fallen asleep at the wheel or had hit black ice on the highway and lost control of the vehicle. Toxicology reports were also being done to determine if alcohol was a factor but those results would not be back for several weeks. Brad had a friend, Sheldon with him that evening. Sheldon had fallen asleep and only awoke when the accident occurred. Physically, Sheldon had suffered only a broken wrist but his emotional damage was much deeper. Sheldon told us that he and Brad had made a split decision at 1 a.m. to go to Ottawa to pick up one of their other buddies from university and bring him back home for the holidays. This plan confused Bruce and I even more because Brad was supposed to come into work the next morning and there was no way that he could have gone to Ottawa and back to Oshawa in time. Brad had never missed work before without talking to us about it first and it was also unusual for him to take a company truck out of town. It seemed that nothing about the whole situation made sense.

The burial was set for December 23. On December 21 we finally got to see him. When I saw him there in the coffin, it became real. I touched him and couldn't take my eyes off of him. I did not want anyone else to see him because that would mean I would have to share him and I definitely did not want to share him with anyone. I wanted to tuck him away in my mind and my heart and keep him all to myself forever. I knew that this thought was not realistic and again put myself on hold and went through the motions of greeting people and just getting through the next few days.

The funeral home was full of people the entire time of each visitation, and we were amazed at the number of friends and acquaintances that came. Many of them had wonderful stories to tell about Brad, and I drank them in and kept them close to me. Monie said the thing that made the most sense. She asked me that if, in the beginning, I had had a choice to have Brad in my life for nineteen years or not at all, what would I have chosen? Anyone who has lost a loved one can appreciate how that person enriched their life.

Someone I didn't know actually remarked that sometimes the Lord sees a person heading for a life of destruction and decides to end that person's life so that they don't have to experience all the bad stuff. Now, I know that Brad was no angel, but this person's words scared the living hell out of me. I wondered what he knew that we didn't know. I spent many hours worrying over that statement. I wondered if Brad had only pretended that he was okay. I worried that maybe he had been lonely and scared. Those words haunted me for years afterward.

There were a few memorable moments during those dark days. Our whole family agrees that Helen is prone to "funeral nerves" because she is nervous at funerals and oftentimes says or does something inappropriate. She was, as usual, the instigator of a little bit of humor. I was sitting beside her when she looked up at two guys coming through the door and said, "Oh my God, there's Lenny and Squiggy" (from the tv show *Laverne & Shirley*). Sure enough, that's exactly who they looked like, and, when I went to greet them, it was hard not to laugh. I almost called them by those names.

The other significant incident was not funny but profound and would have an impact on me for many years to come. It was the night before the funeral. Bruce had taken some of the medication and was sleeping, but all I could do was sit on the loveseat in the living room and think. I was angry, with whom I have no idea, because I had been taught very early on that getting angry with God was not a good thing. I was afraid that if I was angry with God that it would hinder Brad's entrance into Heaven. I talked to God and told him that he had taken all the men that I loved and asked him just when he was planning on taking Bruce. A voice that sounded like Brad's said quite loudly: "Nineteen ninety-nine." This scared the shit out of me, but the answer was nine years away. So I put it out of my head to deal with when I had to. I turned my thoughts to Brad and wondered how on God's Earth I was going to be able to face the closing of the coffin the next morning. I knew that it had to be done, but I did not think I would survive it. As long as it was open, I could look at him and pretend he was just sleeping. I had always had a thing about closed doors when the kids were growing up. I felt that if they woke up afraid in the night, they had enough to contend with without having to open doors. Therefore, our bedroom doors (until the kids were older) were always open at night. On this night, my thoughts were: "What if he needs me? If they close the lid, he'll never be able to get out!" As I was sitting there telling God that I couldn't do this, I couldn't let them close that lid, all of a sudden it was like Brad was beside me. I was wrapped in a giant cocoon of pure love and peace that I can't amply describe, and I fell asleep curled up there on the loveseat. I didn't wake up until early morning, and, when I did, I felt strong enough to get though whatever the day would bring.

Bruce put Brad's watch that we gotten him in Antigua on his own wrist, and he wore it for the next sixteen years. It still sits on his dresser to keep Brad close to him. Brad's coffin was filled with memorabilia from his short life. There were trophies that he gotten from wrestling during his school years, pictures and all kinds of things. He was buried surrounded by wonderful memories to take with him. Kedron Church, where we had been married and where the kids had been baptized, was overflowing, and some of the people had to stand outside during the service. Some of his friends even formed an honor guard at the cemetery.

Everyone came back to our house after the funeral, and I wanted them to be there to keep me occupied but I also wanted them to go so that I could be alone to grieve. Soon enough, everyone was gone, and there was just Bruce and Andrea and me. Bruce's Christmas presents for Brad sat in the shopping bag that they had come home in, and there were all kinds of other presents already wrapped and under the tree for him.

As Christmas day approached, all I could think of was the Christmas before and all the other Christmases when I had told the kids that no matter how old they got or how many children of their own that they had, they would always have to come to our house to stay overnight on Christmas Eve so we could all be together Christmas morning. Until that year, I had always loved Christmas. Now I dreaded the thought of it. Everyone stayed away this Christmas, and the three of us woodenly went through the motions of opening gifts, fully aware that something of utmost importance was missing. I think that if it hadn't been for

Andrea, we would not even have acknowledged the day. I was glad to put everything away and try to bring some type of normalcy to our lives. We talked about Brad a lot, and, every time, the tears would not stop flowing. We encouraged Andrea to see her friends and to do whatever she felt like doing.

One day, a week or two later, she came home in tears and very angry. She had been to the shopping center with some friends and had run into Joanne, a friend of Brad's since they were babies. Joanne's parents, George and Linda, had been our best friends during all those years as well. We had done everything together, including holidays in Florida, cottage rentals on long weekends, and all kinds of things. George and Linda's kids were as angelic as ours were devilish. They never got into trouble, always did well in school, and were the ideal children, while ours were the exact opposite.

Well, when Joanne saw Andrea at the shopping center, she went up to Andrea and told her that she should be ashamed of herself, out having a good time with her friends so soon after Brad's death. Andrea was really upset when she came home, and we had a big talk about it. I told Andrea not to worry about it, and she should do whatever felt right for her. I had barely finished talking to her when the phone rang. It was Linda. I was furious but did not say anything while Linda told me that Joanne was right and that Andrea should not have been out having a good time. I must have made some comments back, but I felt like I had been stabbed in the heart. Here was my best friend saying what I felt were really mean and hurtful things. I'm not sure exactly what she said, but what I heard in my heart was that not only had I lost one child, but the only child I had left was a bad person. Not exactly what a parent needs to hear at a time like this. I made up my mind that I wanted nothing more to do with these people and hardened my heart against them. Bruce didn't see it that way, and we had a few disagreements about it. We saw them a few times after that, but I was not overly friendly. A couple of times when Linda asked me if she had done something, it was in a place where I didn't feel it was a good time to say anything. To this day, they do not know what the problem was. They just think I changed after Brad's death. Today I don't feel any ill will against them, but they will never have the opportunity to get that close to me again.

Three weeks before Brad's accident, we had attended the funeral of a friend of ours who had died of breast cancer. Bruce had been an attendant at their wedding, and, in our early years together, we had hung out with them. It was the first death of one of our peers from the A&W days, and then, just three weeks after Brad's death, Brian Zam, who had come to our door to help that morning on December 19, was killed in a freak accident with a piece of equipment. Our other Brian W was here in the kitchen when I got the phone call, and we both started crying. As we hugged each other, Brian expressed his bewilderment about what was going on with all these deaths. It was a strange time for all of us and confirmed that deaths happen in threes. Only a few weeks later President Bush announced war on Iraq. I don't know why, but this had a huge impact on my psyche. I truly felt that the whole world was changing, and things would never be normal again.

The following are some excerpts from my diaries over the next few years.

November 11, 1991 (on our way home from a much-needed vacation)

As we were sitting outside our hotel waiting for our pickup to the airport, we met a nice couple from Bobcagen. We were just generally talking when she asked me if we had any children. I told her that we had a daughter who would be turning 18 next week and that we had lost our son in a car accident last Christmas. When I mentioned Brad, she then told me that they had lost a son too, about 8 years ago. She then described his accident to me. Her story stayed in my mind, and of course I started picturing Brad's accident all over again. A picture of his head hanging out of the window with the side of his face all cut up and his neck broken had haunted my thoughts for about 6 months after the accident. It was gradually coming to my mind less often, and I was starting to be able to picture Brad normally, but her story started these visions all over again. I tried thinking of other things and reading a book, but sitting on a plane for 4 1/2 hours gives one too much time to think. I ended up crying on the plane and trying to be inconspicuous. I don't think anyone noticed, but for awhile I thought I would just go crazy. I wanted to run and scream and jump out of the plane, and the only thing I could do was to sit there and appear normal. Fortunately, Bruce was sitting a few rows up from me, so he was unaware of all of this.

December 17, 1992

I have been doing much soul-searching along with drawings of my life journey. I am still unable to let go. I have this reasoning that if I forgive myself for my guilty acts, then I will become shallow or arrogant or in denial of my blame. By not accepting responsibility for my role in Brad's life on Earth, I will become less of a person. I will forget and become self-serving—just forgiving to get myself off the hook for these feelings.

I guess in some way my guilt is my badge of honor/cross to bear for not having been a perfect parent. (Or is it a way of eliciting sympathy from the world?)

I need to see.

I need to stand back and be objective.

December 1, 1993

December brings back a lot of memories, especially the bad ones about Brad's death. You know, it's funny—I would have thought that 3 years would give a person time to deal with it and accept it. Well, I haven't done that. If I let myself think about it, I still want to scream, holler, rant, rave, and all kinds of things. It hurts as much now as it did the first year. So I don't let myself think about it. When I go to the cemetery, I still get either angry or numb. The only thing that my mind keeps seeing is what he must look like at the moment, and that picture is not pretty, but rather something out of a horror movie.

December 11, 1993

The other day Bruce handed me a sheet and asked me to check the spelling before he took the article down to the local paper. It was story and poem that he had written for Brad, and it was really beautiful. There were only about 2 spelling mistakes in the whole thing, which tells me that he put a tremendous amount of effort into it. He is the most sensitive and thoughtful man, and I don't think there's anyone else quite like him.

December 16, 1993

My head has been aching constantly and my stomach is in knots. I think it's just nerves with the 19th coming up. How we ever got through these last 3 years, I don't know, but I would not want to go through it again. If only we could turn the clock back to 3 years ago today and stay there forever. I can't accept this, and I can't get angry! I can't get angry with Brad because he suffered enough. I can't get angry with God because that just wouldn't be right. I can't get angry at Bruce because I'm afraid of the consequences and beside it's not his fault. So that leaves me, and I guess I'm angry at me most of the time. I know that anger turned inward is destructive, but my heart won't go any other way. If I cry and Bruce catches me, he gets upset because I'm upset, so I keep an awful lot from him. I know that he goes through a tremendous amount of pain on his own, so how can I possibly inflict more on him? I'm making the best of things the only way I know how, and, if it eventually threatens to destroy me, so be it.

December 18, 1993

Today is the 18th. Little did I suspect 3 years ago when I went to bed that night that life as I knew it would be gone forever before I woke up in the morning. I would give my life to go back to 3 years ago today. I'm going to the cemetery this morning, and I'm going to sit and try to make sense of all of this. I will feel guilty for the rest of my life for not being more in tune to this child of mine. I know that I need to find peace before I can accept his death, and I hope for my own sanity that I can do that soon. My mind tells me that if I accept his death, it means I have to let go of him, and maybe I'm afraid I'll let go of him and never get him back. I do not like talking to anyone about Brad because I hug his memories close and do not want to share him with anyone. He was mine. My son. The one I gave birth to first, the one I loved and fought with, the one who, when the chips were down, would champion for me. I remember going through hard times with Andrea and Brad being so protective of me and trying to help me through my pain. I'll never forget the week before his accident when he was up for supper. We joked about my making spaghetti that night because he was living off of pasta, and the one night he showed up, what did we have—pasta. When he was going home that night, he stood in the front door and gave me a big hug and said, "Thanks a lot, Mom. I really appreciate everything you guys are doing for me." I replied, "I know you do, Brad, that's why we do it." I could have hugged him harder that night. Why didn't I? The guilt continues to build, and yet my mind continues to carry on the negative thinking. If I start to feel good about something, the thought comes into my head: "Don't feel too good or something bad will happen to take it away." You know, it's a terrible thing to think, but in my mind Bruce is going to die anytime and leave me alone just like everyone throughout my life always has. If I build a wall around my heart a little higher, maybe it will withstand all and the hurt won't be able to get inside.

I know that the next few days will be extremely difficult, and, as I write this, my hand, which had become very cramped, suddenly felt warm and comfortable. God, give me the strength to believe that you took Brad because you needed him more than we did. Give me the knowledge that he is with you and watching over us all with a smile on his face and that he is full of happiness. If I know this, I can be happy for him.

December 19, 1993

So much for good intentions. After a frustrating visit to the cemetery, I thought, "F—— it. I just won't think about it. I'll keep myself so busy, and the day will pass and be over." Although I kept busy, my phone also rang with messages of care and concern from our family and friends. Of course, this brought it back into the forefront of my thoughts and got me upset. I do not want to think about it. I do not want to talk about it. I do not want anyone to come and visit and remind me about it. If I don't acknowledge, say, or write any details, maybe it didn't happen. Maybe Brad will show up one day out of the blue. Maybe I'm just having a nightmare. I can't think about it, or I'll go crazy for sure. I have pictures, but I cannot look at them. I should, I know, but I can't. I'm writing about other things now.

April 12, 1994

I've finally figured out that mornings are my worst time of the day. I don't know if I'm having dreams about Brad at night or what, but the majority of my mornings start with a feeling of, "Why bother starting this day?" I constantly have this feeling of impending doom and of something happening to Bruce, and I tend to dwell on it a lot. I've seriously considered suicide but won't do it because I'm a chicken at heart. I'm also afraid I wouldn't go to Heaven, and then I'd never see Brad. The other factors are how hard it would be on Bruce and Andrea.

Although Andrea is 20 years old and quite independent, I still feel she needs me a lot. As for Bruce, I feel guilty leaving him even for 3 hours to go to bingo. Maybe the other reason is that I feel God left us behind for a reason. For me, maybe it was to learn a lesson in suffering or something. I find that every time I have a happy thought or get optimistic, an inner voice tells me I don't deserve to be happy so don't get too excited! I know I have to come to terms with life and death, but, every time I try to think about it, my mind blocks my thoughts. As far as Brad is concerned, he's away for a little while. I just have to be careful because lots of time I find myself about to ask Bruce if he's seen him, and next time he does tell him to come see his mom. If I start thinking any other way, it's like a huge, dark pit of madness begins to open up and swallow me. I can listen to someone talk about him, but it's only a surface thought. I can't let it go further than that. I hear others say something about him, and I don't feel that they have the right to talks about him because he was mine, and I'm not ready to share his memory with anyone. I don't know if I will ever be able to do that.

I will try to come to terms with everything and be positive in my thinking that life is worth living. I keep telling myself that I'm not the only parent that this has happened to. I think about other parents who have lost much more, and I wonder how they go on. Maybe one day I will know that secret as well.

January 18, 2000

It's been more than 10 years since Brad's death, and I still do not trust "good" feelings. It took me a good 5 years before I could think about Brad without having to close my mind. Many times, I thought I would like to end it all and spent a lot of time thinking about how I could do it and make it look like an accident. I thought of stepping out in the traffic on the 401 after running out of gas or losing control of the car and having a fatal accident. At times the fact that Bruce and Andrea still needed me was overridden by the fact that I just didn't want to be in this world anymore. Bruce continues to deal with everything in his own pragmatic way, and Andrea is moving ahead with her life. I had given up all volunteer work and outside activities. Live has revolved around home and the business. In 1995 Andrea suggested I spend some time doing volunteer work with a local YMCA program. I tried it out and did enjoy it somewhat, but something major was always missing from my life. In late summer 1995, everything seemed to come to a head. I went to the cemetery and sat for quite some time, coming to terms with things. It was time! I was either going to get my sorry life over with or find a reason to get on with it. I sat there and talked to Brad, Brian, and God. I discussed with them why I was still here on Earth and not up there with them. The outcome was that apparently they don't want me yet, and I had things left to do with my life. I thought about it for a while and by coincidence got accepted for a course at Durham College that had previously been full. Since then I have taken many other courses and still go to school

2 nights a week. I still have bouts of depression and sometimes the headaches and neck pains are constant companions, but I think I have come to terms with me. I don't think that I will ever again be considered a happy person, but I will be more than pleased to settle for a peaceful person.

Chapter 25
Bruce Forty Already?

Isn't it amazing how we can live in so many different levels at the same time? Maybe this was when I gradually began to look into the idea of giving that voice inside my head a name. After all, it could provide me someone to talk to, confide in, and argue with without seeming like a total nut bar. Having these discussions with another part of myself helped me to help myself. I came to recognize that there were many parts of me active at any given time. There was the wife, mom, and sister, and there were a grieving me, a normal me, a compassionate me, and so on. I could probably go on naming those other parts for a while, but you get the idea.

The compassionate part of me watched Bruce trying to make sense of his world as 1991 started another decade. Bruce continued to go the cemetery everyday without fail. He came to know all of the staff up there and almost became a part of their daily work life. He became acquainted with many of the families that had graves around Brad's. I, on the other hand, could not bring myself to go up at all. It got so that I did not want anyone to even mention Brad's name. If they did, a voice inside me would say, "You can't talk about him. He's mine, and you can't have him." Of course, I never said this out loud, and I became very adept at hiding my feelings. Whenever Brad wasn't being talked about, I could tell myself that he was away and would be home soon. I'd even catch myself thinking, "Brad hasn't called for a while. He'd better call me soon." And then I'd just let it go until the thought came up again. I played this game for almost seven years. In the meantime, I acted perfectly normal. I was aware of allowing Andrea to grow at her own pace and trying not to smother her. Instead, I became her staunchest supporter for whatever she chose to do with her life.

Even though I acted perfectly normal, there were quite a few times when I planned out how to end my own life. I would fantasize about how I could make it look like a fatal car accident. Two things stopped me from going ahead. One was that, with airbags in cars, I might not die, only injure myself and then end up paralyzed or permanently damaged and still have to live, therefore putting more of a burden on Bruce and Andrea. The other thing was that if what I heard as a child was correct, I would never get to Heaven if I committed suicide and therefore never get to see Brad again. These two things were very powerful motivators to keep on going.

In April 1991 Bruce was going to be forty years old. He was still grieving, although handling it quite well, and I wanted to do something special that might give him something else to think about. When Brad had died, we were, as always, cash poor. Consequently, he had cashed out some of his Retirement Savings Plan (RSP) to pay for the funeral, cemetery plot, and headstone. Because I had always believed in equal rights, I thought that I could use some of my RSP's for whatever I wanted. Our friend Ted, whom I had met when we both became Beaver leaders, had a 1989 Corvette that he had purchased about six months earlier. He now had it up for sale, and I knew that Bruce really loved that car. I made arrangements to buy the car from Ted for Bruce's fortieth birthday. Brian, as always, was right there with me, helping me to make it happen. He even had his friend Myron paint a remote control Corvette exactly the same as the real one. I had everything done the week before Bruce's birthday and barely slept in those days before. I had never gone out and spent that kind of money on anything on my own and wavered back and forth about whether Bruce would be upset with me.

I had planned out the whole day, and, on his birthday, when the alarm went off, the radio station played "Happy Birthday Baby" to him. When he got up and looked outside, there were forty penguins sitting on the front lawn. We waited until he was in the coffee shop having his morning coffee with his buddies, and then Brian and Myron drove the remote control Corvette right into the coffee shop and over to his feet. While he was looking at that, I drove the real Corvette around front, all decorated in balloons and a banner. Bruce didn't believe that I had actually bought it; he just thought I had borrowed it for the day. I had to show him the title in his own name before he would believe me. While we were giving him the car, I was having a forty-foot high hot air balloon installed on our front lawn. It lit up at night, and there was a large banner on it that read, "Happy 40th Birthday, you spoiled brat." You could see the balloon that night from about two miles away! I rounded out the day with forty yellow roses, and my niece, Tammy, made a huge cake with a red Corvette on it. We had an open house for everyone to drop in, and, by the time everything was over that day, I think Bruce thought forty was a pretty good thing to be.

Bruce took to that Corvette like a duck to water. For the first year or so, we drove it and enjoyed it. He started to make some modifications to it to make it his own and eventually we joined a Corvette club and began doing shows and cruises and all kinds of great things. Over the years he has received many, many trophies for the car, and we have made some wonderful friendships. That Corvette opened up new avenues in our lives, and now seventeen years later he still declares that he will never part with that car. I guess I had finally done something right for a change!

Andrea finished high school and decided that she wanted to go to college. We tried to talk her into staying in high school for the extra credits for university, but she refused. So we gave in and off she went to college. Although her marks were good, I don't think she did a whole lot of studying those two years. Maybe she needed to be away from us for a while. She graduated from college, still with no idea what she wanted to do, and then decided she should move back home and go back to high school for those credits that she needed for university. This time around, she attended classes faithfully and even had the nerve to ask me why we didn't kick her ass in the first place and make her go to school every day when she was initially in high school. I told her that, short of coming to sit in class with her, there was nothing we could have done.

I used to drive her to school and watch her go through the doors into the school. What I didn't know was that half the time she walking through the school and straight out the other door. This time she was much more serious, hired a tutor for the subjects she was having problems with, and a year later was accepted into the neuroscience program at Brock University in St Catherine's.

As a parent, you always wonder if your kids pay any attention to the lessons you try to teach them. In our case, it was literally years later when something that I had said got thrown back at me. I don't think Andrea realized it, but I sure felt good when she did this because I knew she had listened. One of those lessons happened when she was about fifteen years old. Both of our kids had started with part-time jobs when they were about fourteen. Andrea would go to a job, and, after a few months, everyone would be declared an asshole and she would quit and move on to another job. Finally, one day I said to her, "If everywhere you go, everyone is an asshole, maybe you'd better have a look at who the asshole is." I also told her that no matter where she went in life, there were always going to be people that she disagreed with. I told her that her goal should be to get the credit in that course or to collect a paycheck, regardless of whether she liked the teacher or the people she worked with. I don't think she replied at the time, but she did settle down to stick with school and her job. Years later, when I was relating a story to her about some issues we were having, she repeated back to me word for word what I had said about assholes. I couldn't help but laugh and tell her she was right and it was a nice feeling to think that that lesson had made that much of an impact on her.

The other significant lesson happened when she was at university. We were paying for her schooling, books, lodging, food, and an allowance for personal use. When she complained about being broke, I told her that studies have shown, even in university, students who work twenty hours a week or less do better than students who didn't work, so she should feel free to go out and earn the extra money that she needed. She got a part-time job in a hotel chain in Niagara Falls cleaning rooms. The pay was pretty good, and she could work full-time over the summer to make some extra money. One morning, the phone rang about 6:30 in the morning. When I answered the phone, it was Andrea. Her only words were, "I hate you." Wondering what I was guilty of this time, I asked her what was wrong. She replied, "These damn morals and values that you instilled in me! I hate my job and don't want to go to work, but I'm not sick so I have no excuse to not go into work. Therefore, I have to go to work, and it's all your fault!"

I covered up my amusement with sympathy and told her that it was only for a few months and that it would be over soon. I also told her that doing this job would help to reinforce that she should get her education or she might very well be doing work like this for the rest of her life. After I hung up, I felt so proud of her, and I think I smiled most of the day, realizing that she really was growing up.

In 1991, as the first anniversary of Brad's death approached, I truly thought I was going crazy. We had been through all of those horrible firsts. The first missed Mother's Day, Father's Day, birthdays, and so on. One minute I would be okay, and then the next minute I would be plunged back down into the depths of despair. That first spring, I was sitting out on the back deck. It was a beautiful day, the sun was warm, the grass still that beautiful spring green, the tulips and daffodils were up, and the other plants were just popping through the earth. I sat and closed my eyes and thought how good the sun felt. As I did, into my head popped, "Brad would have enjoyed this day," and immediately I felt guilty for enjoying it. I was constantly dealing with these types of thoughts, and they were driving me crazy. Although eventually they became fewer, they were always close by. As November was getting ready to head into December, I bit the bullet and went to see my family doctor, whom I had not seen in quite a few years. He sympathized with my woes and reassured me that what I was going through was perfectly natural. Even so, he suggested that I might like to see a psychiatrist who could help me. I agreed to give it a try and was given an appointment. I saw the psychiatrist for three visits and came away frustrated each time. I had expected someone who would lead me into conversation and zero in on areas where I might need help. Boy, was I naïve. I would go in and sit, and, unless I said something, he would not say a word. It would have been nice if he would have at least given me some guidelines as to what he expected or what I should expect, considering I was a psychiatric virgin. He did give me a prescription for an anti-anxiety medication, which I had filled but never took. In retrospect, I think subconsciously it was a backup if I decided to go through with ending my life. On my third visit, I was finally cluing in and figured that I would just blurt out whatever came to mind to see if that would open up some conversation, but, after I went in and announced myself to his secretary, the doctor kept me waiting for more than forty-five minutes past my appointment time. Every minute that I sat and waited increased my anxiety level, and I became so worked up that I went into a full-blown panic attack. I started shaking, badly and my mind could only focus on escaping. I ended up running away and never went back. It was not a good experience.

Chapter 26
Death Strikes Again

As time went on, I existed and, for all outward appearances, was normal. The only person who knew how bad my emotional state had gotten was Brian. We spent many hours talking about literally everything and trying to fit some meaning into life. I had even told him about my premonition that Bruce would die in 1999. Then Brian began to experience his own problems. Physically, he began to have some problems with his legs not working properly, and the doctor started him on a battery of tests to determine what was wrong. Although there was never any concrete diagnosis, he was convinced that he had either MS or bone cancer. He became alternately depressed and hopeful, riding this roller coaster until May 16, 1994.

Brian was very much of a perfectionist and did not abide things that did not work right. I think this included his own body, and he felt it was the ultimate betrayal for it to malfunction on him. During this time, he took a buyout from his job at GM and tried to put his affairs in order. Bruce and I feared for him, and, when he had quit his job, walked into our house, and threw the check on the desk, Bruce said to me, "He's planning to commit suicide."

Because it was late spring and his symptoms seemed to be better in warm weather, we felt that we could buy some time and that he wouldn't attempt anything until the fall of the year. Our hopes were that there would be a diagnosis by this time. But those hopes were shattered on May 16, when Brian took his own life, leaving behind a bewildered wife and an eight-month-old son. Because of our talks, I totally understood why he had done it. I didn't like it, of course, but I did understand his reasoning. There were other things going on with him emotionally as well but that is not my story to tell. The day of his funeral, I went to the funeral home very early in the morning and spent about an hour with him. I talked to him, ranted and raved at him, and finally in acceptance I said good-bye. This was my way of coping with his death.

One of the most significant things to come from Brian's death was my thinking about the Catholic religion. We had been taught that taking your own life was a terrible sin and meant you could never go to Heaven. Knowing Brian and what a good and wonderful person he was had me seriously questioning this, and during this time I began to move further away from formal religion and into the spiritual realm. I questioned almost all aspects of my former religious background and began to get a different perspective on God and the afterlife. To this day, my thinking is still evolving, and, in some ways, I can't wait to find out what it's really all about.

Brian's death left a tremendous hole in our lives, and the important men in my life were dwindling considerably. The only male support left in my life was Bruce, and I believed that I only had him for another five years. I was truly convinced that I was paying the price for having taken the life of my grandson when Andrea was fourteen. God himself could not have persuaded me otherwise, and I felt that I must be personally responsible for all the bad things happening in my life. Remember those sins I started racking up as a child? They were continuing to mount! At the same time, I knew that I truly wasn't a bad person, and I tried to live my life to the best of my ability every day. But I figured that I must have had a hell of a lot of atoning to do. The following is from my journal on our twenty-fourth wedding anniversary:

November 21, 1994

I had to stop writing for a bit because there have been some major things that have happened, and one is very difficult to think about, let alone deal with. On May 16, first thing in the morning, the contractor showed up to install the new flooring in our kitchen and hallway. Minutes later, Richard G. called for Bruce and said that he was coming up immediately. They had found Brian dead in his truck in one of their storage units. He had committed suicide. We knew something was wrong but figured he wouldn't do anything until the summer was over. Needless to say, his family was devastated. It was a hectic time, and, through it all, I understood completely why he did it. He had been in so much pain over the past year, and we had talked about it. We had also had a discussion about suicide only the week before. Brian sat here and told me he had been to the doctor and was in the 2nd stage of depression. When I asked what the 3rd stage was, he said "suicide." I thought that was ridiculous, more or less said so, and then changed the subject. If I could turn back the clock to that day, I would do things completely different, but I cannot undo the past and that is another burden I must learn to live with.

We spent all our time at the funeral home and with Brian's family and friends, and I went by myself to the funeral home early on the day he was buried. I went very early in the morning and had him all to myself for an hour. I ranted and raved, laughed and cried, and told him everything I didn't say before he died. I said good-bye in my own way, and I will miss him desperately until the day I die and see him again. He was cremated and his ashes are buried at Thornton, but I cannot feel his spirit there. I can feel that he and Brad are together at our grave site, but, because one half of me still shuts down when I go there, I find it a frustrating and futile experience.

I can't think of one without the other. One is too painful to even think of, and the other (Brian) makes me so bittersweet by making me smile at the goofy memories while my heart is so heavy that I can hardly hold it in my body.

I miss Brad something awful and would gladly give my life to bring him back. But when Brian went, he seemed to take all of my laughter with him. He was the only one I've ever known who could tease me out of a bad mood and make me truly laugh even if I didn't want to. This house is full of him. He built every room, and those 6 months were full of laughter and joy. Maybe because it was the last summer before everything changed forever that makes them seem especially special. I don't know, but I do know that almost all of the men that I've loved the most in this whole world are gone, and, if something happens to Bruce, I'll have no men in my life left.

With Brian, it was a relationship that can never be explained. He had a need to be part of our lives, and we needed him, but none of us ever really knew why. I can see all of us as brothers and sisters in a previous life being very close, and I think that relationship carried over into this life. If this theory is true, I can look forward to us all being together in our next life. In the meantime, I miss him more than I could have believed possible. I miss our lunches together a couple of times a week, I miss him walking into the kitchen in the morning and asking if it's toasty this morning, and I miss him giving me hell for something or other. But most of all, I miss him being outspoken and goofy, making weird noises, or acting with his voice all funny and his goofy expressions and his imitation of people we know. Most of all, I miss having someone on the same wavelength as me. He was my soul mate, and he was Bruce's and my best friend. Don't ask me to explain it. That's just the way it was, and I understand what he did and I think I would do the same thing if life handed me that cup of tea. Brian, I miss you now, I've missed you since May 16, and I'll miss you forever!

It's funny because I can write and think about him with a smile on my face, maybe because I did get to spend that last morning with him and tell him everything. I only wish that I could feel the same with Brad, but I can't accept his death because I can't stop feeling guilty about so many things. I can't accept that he is gone with so much in life ahead of him. I don't want to let him go. I want him to walk through the door and say, "Hi, Mom, where's Dad?" I want to see him happy, get married, have those 16 kids he wanted, and everything else that he wanted out of life.

My salvation will be seeing him when it's time for me to go. Death lives by my side every day of my life, and many days I'm afraid to look over my shoulder because it may be ready to spin me around and take Bruce from me too. I am obsessed with this, and every time Bruce is out of my sight, I'm wondering if someone's going to come knocking on the door to tell me that he's dead.

My laughter is surface laughter, and not much penetrates to my heart these days. I still start to feel joy and immediately stamp it down so that something bad doesn't happen. On the other hand, I try to impress certain things in my memory so that when everything else is gone, I can have memories to keep me going until my time is up.

I don't know if I'm contemplative because it's our anniversary or whether it's the time of year. These are the months that all the major happenings in our life take place, and I dread them coming every year. I am glad when January rolls around. If someone would have told me 24 years ago what life would be like, I would still do it all again, but I would try to be a better person, wife, mother, and friend. I'm learning these lessons but oh so slowly. I think I am becoming a better person, at least on the outside, but inside most times is a little girl who doesn't understand how all this can be happening. I'd better go now, or my whole day will spent in remorse and depression.

By 1995, I had become so sick of the emotional roller coaster that I was riding on that I decided I had to fix my life one way or another. As I had always enjoyed learning and school, I thought maybe I would enroll in some psychology classes to understand what was going on with me. When I went to enroll in the class, it was already full. I took this as a sign that this was not the way for me to go, so in desperation I headed to the cemetery. I spent the afternoon there crying and desperate, angry and frustrated. I ranted and raved at God or whoever might be listening and asked them to help me, because I couldn't go on living like this any longer.

I asked that if I was here for a reason, then help me to find that reason; otherwise, just let me die. I believe that I reached my deepest depth of despair and had nowhere to go but up. I went home totally exhausted and never said a word to anyone, but I had given myself up to the universe and had no idea what would happen. I really didn't give a damn one way or another.

The next day the phone rang. It was Durham College, and they told me that they had an opening in one of the classes. It was Interviewing and Counseling, not psychology, but the girl thought that it might be something I would be interested in. I told her to go ahead and sign me up, and I would be there the next night when the class started. I thought, "What the hell, maybe I will learn why I didn't get anything out of seeing the psychiatrist."

Chapter 27
What's behind This Door?

Unbeknownst to me at the time, it was another door opening. I started this class to figure myself out, and fate intervened. For some reason, I just continued taking courses and studying, and finally, about three years later, I clued in to the idea of getting a college diploma. That was as far as it was going to go, though. I think I just wanted to prove to myself that I was still smart enough to earn it.

Somewhere during this period, I became reacquainted with my interest in hypnosis. Years before, when the kids had been young, I had read a how-to book on hypnosis. One afternoon when we were all lazing around in the family room, I read the script to Bruce and the kids. Although none of them would admit it, I think they did go into a light trance.

I had forgotten all about this, and interest in it slowly began to seep in. I saw an advertisement for a hypnosis course in Toronto and asked Bruce what he thought about me taking the course. The reason I asked was because of the cost. It was a nine-day course, and quite expensive for something that I wasn't planning on pursuing. The answer that he gave me that day made me love him more than ever. He told me that I should do whatever made me happy. I had half expected him to make fun of the idea, and his full support threw me right off balance. So off I went and took the course, becoming a certified hypnotherapist and earning me the right to put CHt behind my name.

During the course I was pushed outside of my comfort zone, and I was glad afterward that I had done it. I began to see how hypnosis could be combined with counseling and have a very positive and therapeutic effect, very different from my psychiatric experience. I also began to think that maybe I could volunteer after I was finished with all my courses and be able to help others a lot better than I had been helped.

Part of getting my diploma in human services counseling meant doing three separate placements of a minimum two hundred hours each. One of our friends from the Corvette Club worked at John Howard Society and suggested that I might want to try there for one of my placements. I thought this was a great opportunity for growth, so I applied, got accepted, and went to work there. The practical experience that I got was invaluable.

Beyond doing group anger management, I was also allowed to do individual counseling and anger management. I felt privileged to be trusted in such a position and learned an awful lot about myself at the same time. When I finished my first placement, I took the required classes and then applied for my second placement with a different part of the John Howard Society. This time I was accepted in the housing end of it. It was good experience, but I quickly learned that this was not the environment for me. Being in someone's living space makes me uncomfortable, like I'm intruding on their privacy. I know that it's a necessary job, but I just felt nosy being there in what seemed like someone else's business. I finished this placement and went back to school once again.

Soon I had only a few classes left and one more placement to get my full diploma. One of the last classes that I took was on addictions. During this class we had to pick a topic and do a presentation for the class. Another girl and I volunteered to spend some time at a methadone clinic to gain some insight into this program. One afternoon we went down to interview the staff there. The co-coordinator explained that she would speak to us as she had time in between patients to explain what they did and how the clinic worked. It was a fairly busy time while we were there, with quite a few interruptions. During one of these times when we were left to own devices, I had to go to the bathroom, so I just ducked into the nearest bathroom without thinking. As I was sitting on the toilet, I happened to look at the wall in front of me and was shocked to see a camera aimed at a very private part of me. After reading the sign over it that stated urinalysis would be monitored, I laughed to myself, modestly covered my front parts, and stayed bent over as I moved to the side away from the camera. Once clear, I straightened up, pulled up my pants, and turned around. I immediately started laughing out loud, because right behind me had been another camera. I must have given a really good view of my rear end as I bent over to get away from the camera in front. When I came out the door, the girl I was with passed me to use the same bathroom. I didn't say a word to her about my experience, and the funny look on her face had us both in stitches by the time we got out of there.

Needless to say, it was a good opening story for our presentation, and I think we got almost perfect marks on it. At class the week after, my teacher told me that he thought it was such a funny story that he had related it to his day classes. So almost everyone in the addictions courses knew about us mooning at the methadone clinic.

My final placement was in a town close by and involved counseling families who had a family member with mental health issues. During my initiation, I was taken to almost all of the available facilities in the area that helped individuals and families in a number of different ways. It was extremely interesting to find out what help is available. It was similar to the first placement, because I was doing one-on-one as well as helping to facilitate group counseling sessions. To my knowledge I made only one faux pas, and, after I explained my reasoning, the clients were very forgiving.

Even during this time of schooling for me and with Andrea maturing into a wonderfully responsible young lady and finally nearing the end of her studies, I could not find peace. As 1999 neared those old negative thoughts began to surface once again. Back when Brad had died, I had what I perceived of as insight into Bruce's death. I had been able to push these thoughts out of my mind for a few years, but all of a sudden that damn year was staring me in the face. Brian had been the only one that I had been able to talk to about this, and, with him gone, I was all alone with these horrible thoughts.

Chapter 28
Who Do You Want Now, God?

At first I couldn't even fathom writing about my thoughts and what I believed to be true about Bruce's death. During stressful times it often helped to write, but this was just way too much to put on paper. I have found that writing helps me to deal with things, but how on Earth could I put a pen to paper about this? Finally, I felt like I either had to write it down or go totally crazy. The following is from my journaling during that year and is a good indication of my thinking almost every hour of every day in 1999.

March 23, 1999
One very stressful situation in my life right now is worrying about Bruce. Nine years ago, when Brad died in a car accident, I was devastated and did a lot of talking to him and to God. One night when I couldn't sleep, I was sitting on the loveseat in the living room and thinking about how a lot of men that I love have been taken away from me by death. I questioned how soon God would take Bruce from me. A voice that I believed to be Brad's said, "1999." That's all the voice said. I worried somewhat, but, with the date being nine years away, I put it to the back of my mind. Over the past year and a half, it has entered my mind frequently. Now it is 1999, and I feel like I'm playing a waiting game. It is on my mind every day now, and this winter, every time he goes out the door, I wonder if he's coming back to me. Needless to say, this is driving me crazy, and I am the only person to know about this. I told Brian about it, back when it happened, and we had talked about it.

But Brian died 5 years ago, and I have never told another soul since. This is also the first time it's been put down on paper.

Over the past 6 months, I have had problems sleeping along with physical problems such as a sore neck, back and shoulder aches and pains, stomach problems, and chest pains. I have been to the doctor twice (after not having been for 9 years) and his diagnosis of my problem is that it is probably caused by stress. I now believe that it is a manifestation of worrying about Bruce and becoming a widow. I feel guilty that I know this (or at least believe it to be true). I do not normally keep secrets about anything important from him, but how could I ever tell him this? I feel somewhat angry for being given this information, but at the same time find myself disassociating from him so that I won't hurt so bad when his time comes.

If 2000 comes and we are both alive and healthy, I will sit myself down and thoroughly rethink where this came from and if my interpretations can be trusted. I am handling this situation by playing a waiting game and telling myself that it is in God's hands. I have to trust and accept what he has planned for us. Ideally, I would like to be able to relax and accept that I do not know when Bruce or myself are going to die, whether it be today or 20 years from now, and to live each day loving each other and being the best we can.

I actually feel better having somehow gotten this out of inside me and projected onto paper. I have been holding this in for so long that it has been eating me up. I hope no one reads this until Bruce and I are both dead and gone. Maybe it will show that I'm a fatalist with a big imagination, or maybe it will prove that God exists and prepares us for the future.

September 10, 1999

I have to put this on paper or go completely insane. I've just spent some time crying because Bruce told me something this morning that appears to confirm my thoughts. I am shaking so badly that I can barely write. Over the past few months I have become totally obsessed and feel like I'm living on the very edge of life. Bruce has been doing car shows all summer, and every time he goes out the door I wonder if he will come back to me. We just came back from Bowling Green, Kentucky, and the morning that we left he had a really bad dizzy spell on the way to Scarborough to meet with other members of the club. I drove from Scarborough to Windsor, which is unusual. We had to stop in London because our brand new Coca-Cola trailer had something wrong with it. There was a cotter pin missing, and we could have lost a wheel and caused a bad accident. This, combined with my worry that something was seriously wrong with Bruce, obviously had my stress level incredibly high. Then, on the way from Farmington Hills to Louisville the next morning, he asked me to drive again. On the way home from our trip, the brakes went on the car. Every minute, all I could think about is "Is it going to happen now?" Every nerve in my body was on alert. I still have not told anyone. I told Gloria that when this year was over I would tell her why I sometimes act weird the way I do. I just couldn't tell her because she tells Jim absolutely everything and I couldn't put that burden on anyone else. We did actually get back safe, and I was here thinking, "Thank You, God, for keeping us safe," but my mind keeps telling me: "The fall months are coming. That's when all the major good and bad things seem to happen in our lives!"

Then, this morning over coffee, Bruce told me he had a weird experience last night just before he went to sleep. He said a silhouette appeared that looked like Brad, and he was beckoning Bruce to him. Bruce joked about it when he told me and said that he told the silhouette, "F—— you, I ain't coming!" As he told me, my entire body went ice cold, and I just sat there totally floored. Then I started to cry, and I was trying to tell him why but couldn't get the words out. I just went to him, and he held me and hugged me. I told him about Ma and how she died shortly after she had a similar experience with Barb, my sister who had died. Bruce told me not to worry, that he had no plans to go yet, but with what I already believe, this is devastating to me. Today he has to go to the Landscape

Ontario office in Milton. Will I lose him today? Lord, help me make it though this day....PLEASE.

September 19, 1999

My heart is pounding so quickly right now that I have to write this down. I'm sitting here at the computer printing up the fall cruise flyers for our club, and the light above my head started blinking like crazy. It hasn't worked for about 3 weeks. At the same time, the dogs are looking out the window, and Bella started to growl. All of a sudden, a warm flush came over me and the thought came into my mind: "This is it."

I am hoping I'm wrong, but I have this overwhelming sense of something being terribly wrong. Bruce left about 10 minutes ago to go over to Glen's, and, without saying so, I know he's heading for the cemetery also. God, let me be wrong again, please. How can I put down what I am feeling? My insides feel as though they are pure liquid, and I can't believe my hand is even steady enough to write this. My life is in turmoil. My thoughts almost every minute of each and every day are repeating: "Is this the day?" I can only pray that my insight is wrong, but until December 31 goes and 1999 becomes a very bad memory that I can laugh about with Bruce, all I ask is that I keep my sanity. You see, yesterday was a really good day. We planned the fall cruise and had a wonderful dinner with Jim and Gloria in Bridgenorth. Next weekend is Andrea's going-away party. This is scary, because every time something bad happens there is a sense of goodness just previous, and there always seems to be a planned get-together. At this point everything appears to me to be lined up for disaster, and I fear each day. This morning I was up at 5 a.m.—couldn't sleep—am I going crazy? I can't believe in God and a hereafter and still discount what I think I know. Right now, every time Bruce goes out the door, I worry and I feel sick until he comes back in. Let me be wrong, please.

October 9, 1999

On top of everything else that's going on here, I am going to school 2 nights a week and have midterms to prepare for this week as well as an upcoming presentation. Maybe 1999 is the year I'm going to be the one dying. With all the stress of the year on me, I'm smoking 2 packs of cigarettes a day, my stomach is constantly in knots, I'm having pains in my chest, and I am not sleeping well at all. This really makes me a pretty screwed up person right at this moment. Even my prayers are half-hearted, and I feel like I'm sinking way down in a depression or at least a deep well that is rendering me a zombie. Lord, help me to get back to my better self.

November 17, 1999

Yesterday, 9 years after his death, a letter from the CPP came for Brad (weird!), and then this morning Bruce tells me he's been having really weird dreams. He says that over the past 6 months he's had a recurring dream of being on the middle floor of a building. He can see up and down to other floors but can't get to them. We tried figuring out the meaning and came up with some ideas, none of which had any indications of fatality. I've all but dismissed the idea of Bruce dying because we only have 6 weeks left in this year and all seems to be going well. Bruce has some sleep problems and often seems tired, but I think it also had to do with the time of year. It's always dreary thinking and worrying about the upcoming winter. I'm not going to write anymore because I don't feel like sharing my thoughts today. Good-bye.

I lived in fear that whole year, and, after awhile, this warped thinking became the norm. At the same time, I would be using those parts of me that were normal and could carry on my everyday life. I began constantly talking to Louie and trying to figure out just what the hell was going on. I also got very fed up with me—or maybe someone with a clearer perspective decided that I needed help. My Gemini personality went into high gear, getting bored with the fear, and needed to take another direction. I slowly and painstakingly began to give my fears to

God or the Universe or whoever else might be listening to the inside of my head. Gradually, I was able to turn in another direction. My thinking became somewhat like Scarlett O'Hara's, and I told myself I'd think about it tomorrow. This turned to "I'll think about it on a need-to-know basis and deal with it when it comes." I guess this is called living in the moment.

Chapter 29
Andrea Gives Us a Scare

That endless decade of the 1990s had finally gone by, and the new millennium came
without any major disasters or illnesses.
Combined with having to rethink everything
that I thought I knew was a tremendous
amount of anger. Sometimes there was a rage
so powerful that I thought it would totally
consume me. It seemed to be a combination
of anger at myself for being so stupid, anger
at Bruce for whatever his role should have
been, and anger at the world in general. After
a few months, common sense prevailed, the bad memories and feelings
started to fade, and I eventually came to terms with myself. Our lives
gradually seemed to settle.

Andrea had achieved her BS in neuroscience at Brock University
and had accepted a job at Stanford University in California in 1999.
She had grown into a very mature and career-oriented woman. She
had wanted to be a coroner since she was about fifteen years old, and,
when she finished at Brock University, we told her that if she wanted to
continue on, she would have to do it on her own. We felt that investing
in six years of post-secondary education was enough. It was time for
us to gather our own financial resources together and time for her to
become totally independent.

She understood this and thought that maybe she would work,
gaining experience for a couple of years and carrying on her education
on a part-time basis. As long as she was working and supporting herself,

she could be free to pursue the rest of her studies at her own leisure. She applied for, had an interview, and was hired at the Stanford Sleep Clinic in Palo Alto, California, which is part of Stanford University. In late August of 1999, she and I flew to San Francisco with all her worldly possessions in five suitcases. Within a week, we had found her an apartment, purchased all the necessities, and set her up in a new and very exciting life. She lived in San Jose that first year and then moved into a shared apartment in Palo Alto, where she would be closer to work. Andrea worked with the pioneers of sleep medicine and made some wonderful friends during her three years there, many of whom she keeps in touch with until this day.

Andrea was able to come home every Thanksgiving and Christmas, and I managed to get down for a visit at least every six months. One time we even convinced Bruce to go down for a visit. Someone else usually went with me, and I got to know San Francisco and Northern California quite well. To this day, San Francisco is one of my most favorite places. It is so alive and picturesque, and I could spend hours just wandering along Fisherman's Wharf and watching the sea lions frolicking in the water or touring around the beautiful countryside and of course the shopping is incredible. One of the times when I went to down to visit with my sister in law, Sheree, Andrea was having some elective surgery done. Those four hours that she was in the operating room were a nightmare. I gave the hospital my cell phone number, and we went out for a while. In the short time that we sat waiting, my mind envisioned every bad thing that could possibly happen. I almost drove myself crazy, and the only way around it was to keep myself occupied. Fortunately, everything went as planned, and she was released and recovered very quickly. As I look back now, knowing what the next few years would bring, I had every reason to be frightened!

I had finally completed the required courses and placements from my part-time studies at Durham College and was eligible to apply for my diploma. It had been over ten years since Brad had left us, and I felt like I was emerging as a totally different person than I had been back then, much like the poem at the beginning of my story entitled "A Poem for Spring." Reading the following excerpt from my journal gave me some insight as to how far I had really come:

January 18, 2000

It has been a bitterly cold month, but we have had a lot of sunshine so it has not been a bad winter at all. Andrea came home from California for a quick visit (2 days), but it was so good to have her here even for that length of time. We talk on the phone at least 3 or 4 times a week, so it doesn't feel like she's that far away at all.

Before I close off, I just want to comment on the scene outside my kitchen window. There a covering of fresh snow on the branches of the trees and on the ground. It is still lightly snowing, and the sun is breaking through. There are about 60 birds at the bird feeder, including 2 beautiful red cardinals. In the apple tree there are about a dozen Mourning Doves sitting on the branches. The whole picture looks like a scene from a calendar. Inside, I am having my coffee, and the 2 dogs are laying on the floor by my feet, sleeping. Darwin, Andrea's cat, is sitting on a chair in front of the window watching the birds. Today I feel pretty good with life!

In 2000 Andrea got a job in Calgary, Alberta. It was more of an administrative position and a good stepping stone into furthering her career. It also appeased Bruce, who was constantly worried about her living so far away. He was happy because at least she would be back in Canada and slightly closer to home. I flew out to Calgary in July, found Andrea an apartment around 17th Avenue, a trendy and very active area in Calgary, and even arranged for the purchase of the new car that she wanted to buy. Everything was set up for her move to go smoothly, which it did.

So in September of 2002, once again I helped her move. I flew to California; we rented a U-Haul truck, loaded up all her stuff, and made the two-day journey to Calgary. The trip was an adventure, as well as a chance for quality time. We thoroughly enjoyed the drive through the Rocky Mountains to Reno, the Salt Flats of Utah, and the Big Sky Country in Montana. We took turns driving, and, when we didn't feel like talking anymore, we listened to an audio book. Overall, it was a great trip. It was cloudy as we crossed the border into Alberta, and

Andrea commented that the one thing that she had missed over the past three years was thunderstorms.

Our friend Carl, whom we have known for many years, was now living in Calgary. When we arrived at the apartment building, he was there to help us unload all of Andrea's stuff. We no sooner had everything into the apartment and had ordered pizza from across the street when it started to rain. Sure enough, it was accompanied by a dandy thunderstorm. I saw it as a good omen for Andrea, welcoming her back to Canada.

Unfortunately, Calgary, although a wonderful city, did not offer what Andrea wanted. Over the first six months, she learned that her job was not as promised, and things got so bad that sometimes she would call me from the parking lot at work just so I could give her some encouragement to get through the day. As things went from bad to worse, Andrea decided to leave, and, for the next few months, she worked only part-time at a local hospital. A friend of hers from Oshawa had moved out to live with her, and, although initially we had thought it was a good idea, things began to go downhill there as well. Andrea finally made the decision to move on and got a job at the University of BC.

Because she seemed to have moved so many times throughout her college, university and working career so far, I told her that this time she would have to make the move on her own. I figured that this time she would have her friends to help her and didn't really need me. We have a friend, Myran, who is in the moving industry. and he was really helpful in getting someone to pick up and have all of her stuff shipped to Vancouver. The moving truck picked up all of her belongings on the Thursday before Labour Day weekend. All that was left for her to do was to pack up what was left, load the car, and head out west. In the days before they were to leave, her friend that was living with her wavered back and forth about going. Finally, the day before they were leaving, Andrea's friend decided that she was going to stay behind. There were many things that we didn't know were going on with Andrea. We knew that she was under a tremendous amount of stress about her friend and her employment. She phoned me at least four times on that Friday, sometimes crying and other times just totally stressed out. Finally, she left without her roommate, but with another friend that she had recently met up. She and Brad had known Kyle and his brother in high school, and they became reacquainted when Andrea was home in early August. He had been having some personal problems and felt that a total change might help him to get himself straightened out, so had headed out west also and met up with Andrea. He had decided that he would head to BC with her.

They left Calgary on Saturday morning, and, when they arrived in Vancouver on Sunday, Andrea called us to tell us that she had made it safely and gave me the address where she would be. Because it was the long weekend, everything was closed, so they were just going to take it easy for the next two days. She had an appointment at noon on Tuesday to tie up loose ends for her new job and then would have to look for a place to stay. For the first time in many months, Andrea sounded optimistic and talked about starting the courses that she wanted to take as soon as she got settled into her job.

All that Labour Day weekend Bruce kept teasing me. He would ask me if I felt guilty about not being there to help Andrea move this time. I would retort that it should have been his turn, and why wasn't he out there for her? Neither one of us felt all that bad because we knew that Myran was taking care of her furniture and had even offered to have it stored until she found an apartment. She had Kyle with her, so we felt that she would be okay.

We went to bed on Sunday night and had just gotten to sleep when the phone rang around 1:00 AM. It was Andrea. She told us that she was at the hospital and that they were planning to keep her there to run some tests. She also told us that the staff at the hospital thought that she might be having TIA's or mini-strokes and wanted to have her checked out. She was adamant that they had better have everything completed and let her out before noon the next day, because she was to have her final interview and get all of the paperwork filled out for her new job. She seemed perturbed by the interruption to her life, but otherwise was fine.

As soon as I got off the phone, Bruce said to me, "You're going out there, aren't you?" to which I replied, "Of course." I immediately got on the phone and made plane reservations for the first plane out, which was 9:00 AM. Because at this point I did not have a secretary in our office and it was a payroll week, I did payroll immediately and prepared things for being away. I quickly packed, and Bruce took me to the airport for my flight. I arrived at Vancouver Airport around 11:00 AM their time, and I took a cab straight to the hospital. When I inquired about Andrea, the staff at the Lyons Gate Hospital sent me up to the NCCU (critical care unit).

I couldn't figure out why they were sending me there, probably because my mind couldn't conceive that this was serious. But when I walked into the room where Andrea was, it hit me like a ton of bricks. She was lying in the hospital bed with tubes and a machine hooked up to her body and was totally helpless. I ran over to the bed, got in beside her, and the two us just cried and cried. She had suffered two severe strokes since I had spoken to her, her left side was totally paralyzed, and she couldn't talk. It was devastating, and the phone call back to Bruce to report on her condition was another one of those calls that I had hoped to never have to make.

The doctors and staff at the hospital were absolutely amazing and totally supportive. They looked at every angle of her case and performed numerous tests to figure out what had happened. The nearest thing that they could find for the cause was that she had a hole in her heart. Apparently, everyone is born with this, and most times the hole heals over by itself. But in this case it hadn't healed over and had gone undetected for the first twenty-nine years of her life.

I managed to get a hotel room close by and went to pick up Andrea's car so that I could have some mobility. Over the next few weeks, I spent hours at the hospital with Andrea and on the phone with Bruce. Bruce and I were both trying to figure out what life was handing us now, and being so far apart was incredibly difficult.

While I was at the hospital, it wasn't so bad because I was kept busy meeting with the doctors and other personnel who were helping me sort out medical coverage, the support that I would need, and trying to keep Andrea's spirits up. But when I left the hospital, it was only me, and those old fears reared their ugly heads. I would call Bruce and report on what was happening, and the rest of the time I spent trying to make sense of everything. I had nightmares almost every night, consequently not getting a lot of sleep and worrying about what the future held for Andrea.

I also had the responsibility of running the office at home, so, after a week or so, I made arrangements for Bruce to fly out and stay with Andrea while I flew home and caught up on invoicing and payroll. I picked him up at the airport, and we went straight to the hospital so that he could see her. I don't think he was totally prepared to see her as helpless as she was, and it was a shock to him. Bruce uses humor when he gets uncomfortable, and, as Andrea has the same sense of humor, it was really good for her to have him there.

We spent the night together, and I don't think either of us got much sleep. The next morning he took me to the airport so I could fly home. I came home and worked for three days solid, catching up on everything. Then I flew back out to Vancouver, and the following day Bruce flew back home to Oshawa.

It was becoming increasingly obvious that it was going to a long haul for Andrea's recuperation, and there were no guarantees that she would ever fully recuperate. In the meantime, we also realized that we couldn't continue to keep flying back and forth and stay in hotel rooms. I worked with some people at the hospital in Vancouver to figure out how we could get her back to Oshawa to convalesce. The people at the hospital understood our thinking. Their main concern was to get her stabilized to travel back to Oshawa. On the other end of things, there were no beds available in Oshawa. It was a waiting game on both sides.

During this whole time, Andrea's independence and dignity was tested to the max. She hated the whole idea of being totally dependent on someone else to do everything for her, and, with her speech being so impaired, it was difficult a lot of the time to make out what she was trying to tell us. It was an extremely frustrating time for all of us. At one point she said to me that this is not the way it was supposed to be. It should be her sitting at the bedside of Bruce or me after one of us had a stroke. I agreed with her but also told her that our family just did things differently. After all, in a perfect world, your kids do not die before you either.

Finally, the hospital in Oshawa was able to accommodate Andrea, and we made arrangements to get her back to Ontario. An ambulance would take her to the airport, and then we had to fly first class, accompanied by oxygen. Things went fairly smoothly until Bruce and another ambulance met us as Toronto Airport. As soon as Andrea saw

Bruce and the ambulance team, she started crying uncontrollably and begged us to just take her home. It had been almost a month, and she had had enough of hospitals and therapy. Of course, that didn't happen, and we followed the ambulance to Oshawa Hospital and got her settled in.

Over the next week that she was there, her therapies were constantly being cancelled or just not happening. So we spoke with the hospital personnel and arranged to bring her home, promising that we would take her each day for physical and speech therapy. We were learning firsthand how frustrating our medical system had become. The next year was spent fighting to get her medical treatments, doctors, and the surgery that she would need to correct the hole in her heart. That surgery finally took place three years after her strokes! My negative opinions of doctors and the medical system had once again been reinforced.

Chapter 30
Picking up the Pieces Again

After I had finished my college education and gotten my diploma, I hadn't really thought about doing much with it. I had the idea in the back of my mind that I would like to keep up my skills by having a few clients, mostly for hypnosis. With this in mind, I had converted Andrea's bedroom into an office for myself. Bruce had gotten the idea that if I put a sign out front, I might be able to attract some clients. So I put up a sign, and, sure enough, I began to have a few clients. With Andrea moving back home, everything else was put on hold, and I focused on getting her well and keeping the office of our main business going.

Going through those few months of hell made me realize that whether I wanted it or not, I needed help. I became obsessed with the idea that we needed someone to work in the office who would be familiar with the business. After all, the way our life was turning out, I couldn't always count on being available. What if something happened to Bruce or me? At least if there was someone in the office, it would free me up to look after other things without worrying about our guys getting paid or the invoicing getting done. So I hired and trained Rhoda to look after the everyday office tasks. To this day, I still have a hand in running things, but it's great to be able to count on things running smoothly if I'm not there. I don't know if this was instinct setting in or just good planning, but God wasn't through with me yet and decided to give me some more life lessons.

Andrea gradually regained her strength but has never really gotten her speech back to what it was before the strokes. Within three months of having the strokes, she was capable of working and got a job with a local doctor who had a sleep clinic about an hour or so away. Because she couldn't drive, one of us would drive her to work. She worked three, twelve-hour shifts, and, because it was such a distance, the doctor paid for a hotel room close by. Then we would pick her up again at the end of the three days. She worked there from late November until the following August. It was the first time in years that I did not drive an SUV, and, many times over that first winter, the roads were so bad that I would have given anything to have a four-wheel drive again.

Andrea also took the train to Montreal for a weekend and meet her friends for her thirtieth birthday that November. She wasn't 100 percent but was determined to maintain as normal a lifestyle as possible. She lived with us for that first year, and in August of 2004 gave her notice at the sleep clinic. She had been accepted to UOIT, a local university, to continue her education. Unfortunately, she had a hard time keeping up with the pace of university and withdrew after a few weeks. The university was very good about refunding her fees, and she got a job at another hospital in the Toronto area, but a little closer to home. She worked there and finally was able to get a full-time job at a local sleep clinic where she is currently employed. She also still works the occasional shift in the Toronto hospital.

After that first year at home, it was apparent to Andrea as well as Bruce and me that it was time for her to have her own place. We did a lot of looking, and finally she found a nice home in an older, established neighborhood. It's one of those quiet tree-lined streets where most of the homes have verandas out front and you can sit out and enjoy the peace and quiet, while at the same time she is within walking distance of work and downtown. She has settled in quite nicely, and, as is typical with Andrea, she rents out one of the bedrooms. I think she just likes having someone else in the house with her. She talked about wanting a little dog, so one day when Bruce was out, he bought a three-month-old teacup Pomeranian. It was on my birthday, and he brought the dog home without saying anything to Andrea. When she came in through the door and saw the dog, her eyes lit up. She went straight to him, picked him up, and was not about to let go of him. Bruce kept teasing her that the dog was my birthday present, but she refused to believe him, renamed the dog Mendel, and took him home with her.

He has been her constant companion ever since, although it seems that Grandma and Grandpa babysit an awful lot!

The years of 2003 and 2004 had changed our lives dramatically once again, and then finally it seemed like things were settling down again. Amid everything else, I believe I was entering into the menopausal phase of my life, although I really didn't have a lot of time to think about it.

I started working in my practice again, and, with Rhoda working in the office, felt like we were getting back on track. I didn't notice that I was exhibiting some unusual behavior, but I guess Bruce and Andrea did. I am normally an easy-going person, but it seemed like I was constantly bitchy and on edge. I also seemed to be getting klutzy, and Bruce decided to take matters into his own hands. He had Rhoda make me a doctor's appointment for a checkup. I kicked up a fuss and protested right up to the last minute, but finally gave in and went for the sake of peace in the family. Our family doctor is wonderful, and, when we had first gone to him years before, I had told him that I wasn't one for annual checkups and that I knew my body better than anyone else. My thinking was, and still is, that doctors are for sick people. I firmly believe that if you pay attention to your body, it will tell you if something needs attention.

I went for the checkup, refused some of the tests, and was okay with a general checkup. My blood tests came out fine when I went back for the results, and the outcome was that if I quit smoking and lost 15 pounds I would be in really good shape. Just before I went in for the results, Bruce asked me if I had told the doctor about my brain tumor. As the specialist that I had been seeing hadn't been practicing for the past ten or so years, and with everything else that had been going on I had forgotten all about the tumor. Our family doctor was also new within that ten-year period and did not have our old records. I told Bruce that I had forgotten all about it but promised to mention it to the doctor when I went in.

After we went over the results, I told the doctor that I wasn't sure if it was relevant or not, but I had been diagnosed with a brain tumor years before. He seemed to think it was pretty important and immediately ordered a CT scan and an appointment with a neurosurgeon at St. Michaels Hospital in Toronto. Within three weeks, I was sitting in the specialist's office, looking at my tumor on the computer screen. As my former records were not available for him to compare, he asked me questions, tested my reflexes and strength, and could only tell me what symptoms to be aware of. He didn't seem to be overly concerned and suggested that I return in a year.

I went home with an "I told you so" attitude toward Bruce and Andrea, but was secretly resentful that I had gone through all of those tests and wasted my time on something that I already known: I was fine! I put it all behind me, and once again vowed that I would do things my own way. No one was going to force me into those things again.

My sister Lois was dealing with breast cancer and the subsequent treatments. We dealt with this and all the other changes that were going on, and then, finally, it seemed as though things were settling down again Then, on March 4, 2005, our family was again thrown into shock. My brother-in-law Ken died suddenly of a massive heart attack at work. My sister Betty became the first widow in the family, and it was a real wake-up call. Even now, a few years later, when the whole family is together, I look around and think, "Who's next?"

The day after Ken's funeral, our nine-year-old dog, Kramer, who Bruce considered his "other" soul mate, became ill with a mysterious illness. After about two weeks of trying different things, we were given a diagnosis. The outcome was that he had to be put down. Our vet, whom we have known for many years, came to the house to treat him each day, and, when it was time to say good-bye, we put up a table in the front hallway, and both Bruce and I held him as the vet administered that final shot.

Less than two weeks after Ken's death, my second oldest brother Joe also died of a heart attack while sitting at his kitchen table. As they were in Florida at the time, Gail, Joe's wife, decided to have him cremated and to wait to have a service later when all their friends and family would be back in Canada for the summer.

The deaths of Ken and Joe were the first deaths in the family since Brad had died, and all of a sudden I was again experiencing the feelings and scary thoughts associated with the death of someone that you love. I had been thrown back into the negativity pool, and I guess I was having a harder time than I thought. As I look back, perhaps those old thoughts and fears were worming their way back into my psyche. In March my journal entry described what I was feeling:

> *If you're anything like me, from time to time you attempt to tidy things up and put like things together. I have one of those plastic bags with the zipper that my duvet came in. Of course, I'd probably never put the duvet back in it, but, nevertheless, it's too good to throw out, so I utilized it in one of my tidying frenzies. I decide to use it for techno cables that were left over from things around the house. It is now full of numerous pieces of TV cable, satellite cable, telephone wire, leftover printer cables, adapter wires, and anything else that resembles a cord and is not currently useful. The reason I mention this, is because this morning at 4:30 a.m. I was sitting outside having a smoke and made the analogy between this bag of wires and my mind. This difference is, in my mind, the cables are not all rolled and neatly tied. They are loose and very, very jumbled!*

One of the notable outcomes of my earlier visit with my family doctor was that he was concerned that my mental state was not as good as my physical state and had suggested a prescription for Zyprexa and an appointment with a psychiatrist, which I reluctantly agreed to. My psychiatric outcome is journalized as follows:

> *It's Sunday night, May 1, 2005, and, as I have just had an eventful week, I thought that I would try and put down on paper some of my feelings and the emotions involved. Last Tuesday I had an appointment with our family doctor to renew a prescription that he had given me for Zyprexa, an antipsychotic medication. I started this medication one month ago because I was having mood swings, not sleeping properly, and had also had a few dizzy spells. Following a physical checkup, including a CT scan for a brain tumor that was discovered years ago, my doctor diagnosed me as physically healthy with the possibility of a mild form of bipolar called dysthimia. He seemed to feel that the medication would calm me somewhat and help me to sleep. He also took the precaution of having me*

see a psychiatrist to confirm the diagnosis. I had one visit with the psychiatrist and was due to see him again on Thursday. My family doctor had renewed my prescription with the option of having the psychiatrist take over future renewals.

I was a little nervous about seeing the psychiatrist but also optimistic that our 50 minutes together might produce some insights to help me let go of some of the garbage from the past. I had felt that the first appointment had gone well, and, after refusing further medication (an antidepressant), he seem to understand that I wanted to work out my problems and get the root cause instead of masking it with medication. He then advised me to purchase the book Feeling Good: The New Mood Therapy. I did this and had worked through about four chapters. This book's focus was on cognitive therapy and looking at dysfunctional thinking. Boy, was that right down my alley!

When I went to my last appointment, the good psychiatrist had reverted to strongly advocating an antidepressant. When I asked what purpose the medication would serve, he replied that it would help me bring happiness into my life. I questioned if it would be a false happiness because it was chemically based and would not address the root of the issues that plagued me. He agreed with me in theory and then told me to carry on with the book and come back in six weeks. The appointment lasted less than 20 minutes. I left his office, somewhat taken aback and wondering where things had gone wrong. I had the strong impression that if I was not into taking the medication, he did not really feel that I wanted help. All the way home, I wavered between thought such as "I was right all along, you can only count on yourself," "He doesn't really care," or "I'm not important enough to help." In between these thoughts, I attempted the advice from the book by telling myself, "This is just your dysfunctional thinking," and "The doctor was only doing what he was trained to do. He is trained not to take on your problems," and so on. Because these thoughts were going round and round in my head, I thought that I would try to put them in some type of order, so I turned on the recorder in my car and tried to voice what I was thinking. When I played it back for myself, I sounded like a whiny baby! It really was an outstanding example for me of how, when thoughts go round in your head, they make sense to you, but, when you put them out there into words, they sound lame and distorted. Somehow, I can write about my feelings much more accurately than I am able to express them verbally.

In any event, I proceeded home and thought, "To hell with Dr. ——. I can do it on my own. I'll fix myself!

Chapter 31
Returning to Childhood for a Brief Visit

At the end of April in 2005, my sister-in-law Gail was ready to have a funeral service for my brother Joe. It was to be held at Stoco Church, where our religious upbringing had started. We left Oshawa early in the morning to attend the funeral service. Just driving up to St. Edmund's Parish was like going back in time. In my mind I could see Mona and me and all of the relatives milling about, with the kids coming out of the church on Sundays from Catechism classes and being allowed to play for a bit while the adults visited. I could even see us trying to avoid the aunt who always wanted a hug and to give us the humbugs from the bottom of her purse. With these visions running through my head, we entered the church. For the next while, my mind was a mixture of images as I wavered between paying attention to the service and checking out the beautifully colored windows and the statues around the church that were so familiar. In my mind I could almost see Father Briceland hovering around the altar saying Sunday Mass.

Leaving the church and proceeding over to the Parish Hall was another memory flick. Visions of Mona and me as young girls twirling our batons on stage for Grandma Masterson's birthday, attending CYO dances at about twelve or thirteen years old, all giggly and flushed with excitement about meeting up with boys. Even the smell of the place was familiar, but the one thing that was missing was the hallway to the left of the stage that led back to the old outhouses. Instead, there was an addition on the side of the hall with an updated kitchen and new bathrooms with flush toilets. I guess some things do have to change!

It was fitting and felt good to go with our sisters and brothers behind the hall to visit Ma and Daddy's graves. Lois led us in prayer, and, as usual, Helen, even at sixty-two years old, was still the disruptive one. But that's okay, because long ago we diagnosed her with funeral nerves.

Following the reception at the hall, Gail invited us back to her place for a visit, which we wanted to do, but first I had a mission. I wanted to take a drive down memory lane and explore some more of my childhood. When I mentioned the idea, Mona was on board, along with Jillian, Mona's daughter, Richard and Bruce (our husbands), and we even managed to coerce Lois into coming with us in case we couldn't find our way back.

As we followed the curving roads past familiar places, including our school, and headed toward our old farm, we had to pass Jenny Johnston's place (remember the poor old lady that Monie and I had thought was dead?) As no one was living on the farm now, we talked Richard into pulling in the laneway. The house was deserted, and pretty dilapidated with all the windows smashed out and huge weeds growing all over the place. Although it looked like it was about to fall down at any minute, Monie and I saw none of that. We couldn't get out of the vehicle fast enough, and it was as though Jenny herself was calling us to come in. Even now, as I think about it, I have to giggle to myself. Here we were, two fifty-something ladies all gussied up in dresses and high heels wandering about as if we were children again in our shorts and running shoes. There was junk everywhere, and hundreds of books thrown around on the floor, piled almost ankle-deep, and some of the ceilings were falling in, but neither of us saw it quite that way.

Jillian came in with us, but we hardly realized she was there. We waded through the first floor, amazed at how much of it was exactly as we remembered. We were stopped in our tracks when we walked into one room, and there against the same wall was the same couch that Jenny had been laying on that day. I could see her there as plainly as the day it happened! We took our time going through the rooms and were flabbergasted by the number of books thrown all over the place. Some of the books were very old, and some had letters in them dating back to the early 1900s. As both Mona and I are book lovers, it was heartbreaking to see them so carelessly thrown around. It was as if someone had gone through them looking, perhaps for money and not finding any, and just tossed them on the floor!

We braved our way up the staircase at the end of the house, and what we found upstairs was much the same. There were a few old horsehair mattresses and many more books and letters. In one of the bedrooms, two fur coats were hanging on hangers. They had obviously seen much better days, but Mona was totally intrigued with them. I think if she had been a little less of an honest individual, she would have taken one with her; not that anyone would have cared if she did, because the place had been totally abandoned.

I have no idea how long we were in there because we were so enthralled, but Lois didn't see it that way. She waited in the van with Bruce and Richard and couldn't figure out what the fascination was all about. Finally, they were able to coax us out, but we couldn't resist bringing a few souvenirs with us. We each picked out a few books so that we could have a memory of our visit; however, I don't think we will ever need books to remember. To this day I can close my eyes and recall almost every step in vivid detail. I'll bet that Mona feels much the same way.

We carried on with our drive past our old farmhouse and some of the other rural areas and eventually ended up at Gail's house to join the rest of the family in reminiscing about Joe. Although it was a sad occasion, I think Joe would have been happy to know what a gift he gave us that day that we went to his funeral. A few days after this, I was, for some unknown reason tossed once again back to negativity. I only wrote in my journal once during this time:

May 5, 2005

It's 2:25 in the afternoon, and I have to say, today I feel pissy. That's a new word I learned recently from Betty, who just became the first widow in our family, but that's another story for another time. Right now it's about me, and sometimes, I think too often, it's about me. Other times I think it's never about me. Anyhow, there's nothing particular happening today. Since yesterday, I have been having strange, little pangs in my head that are driving me absolutely crazy. I am also feeling somewhat disconnected, as though I am moving under water. Added to that, I am battling negative, dysfunctional thoughts, such as "I can't be bothered," "Maybe I shouldn't even bother anymore," and so on. What is this dark gray cloud that hangs over my head? It's not quite black, but it is very dark. Yet I have nothing to be sad or morose about. I have a wonderful husband, a great daughter, and family and friends who are supportive. So what the hell's my problem?

One of the things that I've noticed is that the more depressed I become, the more money I spend. I know that money and things do not bring happiness, yet I continue on this defeating path. It really does seem like just too much effort to keep going. Talk about mood swings. As I write this, I am also telling myself "Smarten up, all you have to do is JFDI (just f——— do it!)." "No one can do it for you. You want a better body? Well, get off your ass and on to your feet and move."

Okay, I'm going now. I don't want to talk about this anymore.

Maybe writing this was a bit of a catalyst into motivating me to move on. I continued working with the book that the psychiatrist had recommended and started to consciously make myself look at life realistically and with gratitude. It's been a long hard road, but I think that I have managed to dispel a lot of the negative thinking over time. I also believe that working with clients has helped me to put things into perspective. Maybe it was menopause, and I've come through the other side of it. I don't know, but what I do know is that I'm thankful that those thoughts are mostly behind me. I find now that if they start up again, I'm in a much healthier mental position to fight them.

My only other journal entry since then did not happen until 2007, after I had started on the road to writing this book. This time it was the challenge of putting some of the most difficult times of my life into words:

March 18, 2007

I am the biggest procrastinator in the world. I haven't been doing as much writing as I should, and Bruce even encouraged me by buying me a new laptop for Christmas that is absolutely awesome. Since then I have made token efforts, but time is running short, so I have made up mind to get to work on this book. I am at the part of winning the JDRF money and am really having a problem moving on. I have had chest pains, shortness of breath, negative thoughts, and all kinds of other shit, and I think I've finally figured out what's going on. I am getting to some of the really difficult parts of my life, and I think I'm putting it off because it's going to bring up some painful stuff. I was like this when I wrote about my early teenage years, and I survived those, and I know I will survive the next part. I also know at the other side of it is good times once again. As usual, when I put something down on paper, it gives me that reality check that I need, so wish me luck. —Dorothy Louise

Chapter 32
Does Hypnosis Really Work?

My counseling and hypnosis practice was doing well, and I was as busy as I wanted to be, working two days a week. There was another hypnotist, Lauren Lamont, practicing in the area, and she had sent me some younger clients because she did not work with adolescents. One day I phoned her to thank her for the referrals, and, during our conversation, we agreed to get together for coffee. When we met, we hit it off, and, as I told her about my plans for the upcoming World Hypnosis Day (WHD), she stated that she would be interested in participating with me. By the way, World Hypnosis Day is January 4. It is an opportunity to bring awareness of the benefits of hypnosis, and many hypnotists offer free seminars or sessions so that anyone can see that it is a very natural and relaxed state without all the weirdness that some people associate with hypnosis.

We agreed to get together again and discuss it. Shortly after that, Lauren took a course in Toronto and met another lady who also lived in the area and who also expressed an interest in our World Hypnosis Day plans. Her name was Peggy Kelly, and I met her once before WHD. There was a mutual comfortableness between the three of us right from the beginning. We started having lunch at each other's house every couple of months, and it was a great avenue to keep up-to-date on what was happening in the hypnosis world. We are all open to new ideas and learn a lot by bouncing ideas off each another. We also came to realize that our values and ideas about the benefits of what we do were very similar. It had nothing to do with monetary gain; it was the sense of satisfaction that comes from a client who has achieved something for themselves that they could not have done otherwise!

At one point we joked about giving ourselves a name and becoming a famous trio of middle-aged women who do stage hypnosis. I suggested using the first two letters from each of our names and came up with Lapedo. They immediately thought it was a great idea, and the Lapedo Group became reality. We now do trade shows, advertising, and World Hypnosis Day as a group. It's also great because we can refer clients to one another, depending upon who can meet the client's needs the best.

There are a few notable experiences that I had with hypnosis that helped me to realize what a valuable tool it can be for issues and change. Years ago, not too long after Brian died, I heard about a lady who was experienced in past-life regression. Her office was in Toronto, but, because she lived in Oshawa, she agreed to see me at her home. I went without any expectations and ended up on a roller coaster ride of discovery and enlightenment. I was there for three hours and experienced four past lives. The main things that I learned was that Brian was one of my guides as well as my husband in one life; Bruce has been in three of my past lives, always as a friend because I was a male in those lives; and I also learned that I hadn't been a parent in any of those lives either. I guess that explains why I had such a hard time being a parent in this one—I have no experience!

The second incident came about as a result of my nephew Jonny coming to work for us. Both of Mona and Richards sons, Ryan and Jonathon, worked for us for a few summers. Jonny was a reptile lover and had reptiles of one sort or another all of his life. There were twelve years that I refused to even go visit Mona and Richard because there were snakes in the house.

Because they live two hours away from us in Woodstock, Ontario, the boys stayed with us during the summers that they came to work in Oshawa. When Jonny came to work for us, we had a conversation about no reptiles, and he agreed because he knew how I felt. However, for some reason, the first few days that he was here, I was thoroughly convinced that he had brought a snake with him. I didn't want to ask him, because I trusted his word. I refused to go into his room to check because that would also be betraying trust, so I decided it was time to do something about it. I made an appointment with the instructor where I had taken my original hypnosis course, and off I went to confront my fears.

When I spoke with the hypnotist, I assured her that I knew where the fear had come from and shared the incident from the farm when the snake had wrapped around my leg. Her only comment was, "We'll see," and then she led me into hypnosis. As we regressed back to that first time when I became frightened of snakes, can you imagine my surprise when I moved right past that incident and back into another life? I was, I believe, in Gettysburg, a young male walking through the woods with my group, which was fighting the Civil War. As we were walking along the pathway, I tripped over a tree root and fell right into a nest of copperhead snakes. I was bitten by those snakes many times and died as a result of the bites. As I began to relive this horrifying experience, the hypnotherapist allowed me to rise above it without the emotion and just observe. She then led me through the healing and understanding process, and I came away with a much different perspective. The strange result or lesson from this was that I had died in shame—out of stupidity by tripping and falling, and not in an honorable manner by being shot or otherwise killed in battle.

The outcome of the session was that I no longer worried whether Jonny had brought a snake with him. I trusted his word and was able to let the matter go. To this day, I still do not want a snake wrapped around me or brought into a room where I am, but I am able to look at them on television and I no longer avoid the garden for fear of seeing one.

I have been hypnotized several other times and continue to use self-hypnosis as a powerful tool to understanding what is going on inside my head. I highly recommend it to work through many types of issues.

Chapter 33
More Life Lessons

The year 2006 rolled around with life being pretty good. Andrea was in a stable position with her employment and her personal life, Bruce and I were in good shape, and, for the most part, a lot of the old, negative thinking patterns had all but disappeared. I was finding that being in my fifties was not so bad after all. I finally realized that the only person I had to really worry about liking me was *me*, after all. I had finally gotten the concept, and now I try to impart that knowledge to my clients as often as I can. I realized that if I accepted myself and didn't take myself too seriously, then other people seemed to feel the same. It's a simple concept really, but why in the heck is it so hard for us to grasp?

I was doing well physically and mentally, and I began to think that life was meant to be lived, not observed. Then I discovered something else about myself that I was unaware of. I began to realize that the so called self-help syndrome was there for the taking. Up until this point in my life I had invested in almost every self help book that's been published thinking it would fix me. It's like buying a treadmill and putting it in your bedroom. It only works if you choose to work it! It's the same thing as reading all those books - call them the 'treadmills of the mind' if you will. They are just a knowledge tool. Your mind has to comprehend that in order to actually fix yourself you have to do it yourself and it's much easier when you have the right tools. I have learned to use the power of visualization and positive thinking. Then I just hoped that God or the Universe would hear me. The other thing I learned was that I am as prone to the power of suggestion as much as anyone else.

I had to go for my annual CT scan and then see the neurosurgeon for the results. When I went into his office, there was the previous picture of my tumor beside the results of my latest one. He reported that the tumor appeared to have grown, and that, if the pattern continued, it was possible that I might need surgery in the near future. Apparently, the tumor is in an area in which they do not like to operate unless they truly have to because of the permanent damage it could cause to parts of my body. He thoroughly went over the warning signs and suggested that, if I experienced any of them, I should come to the hospital immediately.

I left his office in a bit of a daze with visions of helplessness slamming around in my head. In a year, I could be less of a person. These visions and the accompanying thoughts threw me back into panic mode, and sharing them with Bruce was both good and bad. He went into his own version of panic mode and began treating me like an invalid, wanting me to take it easy and watching my every move. With the doctor's words resounding in my brain and with Bruce's actions, I fell right into the invalid role. I became intensely aware of my movements if my balance wasn't perfect when I walked across the room. I noticed every muscle twitch, every little ache or pain, and was constantly testing my left side for any signs of weakness. This went on for about a month, and then Louie stuck his two cents in. My Gemini personality had once again gotten bored with the role, and I decided to take matters into my own hands. I gave myself a year to wrap up the unfinished details in my life. That's why, earlier in my story, I stated that I needed to get this done.

I decided that I wanted to get my life story in writing within that time frame. I had also taken a Reiki I course and decided that I needed Reiki II so that I could use the healing power on my tumor. I asked my clients who had Reiki training to do healings for me. Whenever I could find the time, I spent hours on self Reiki and also purchased the *Dreamhealer* books and DVD and did the exercises in visualization that were provided. I went to see Adam (*Dreamhealer*) and came away very impressed with the information that he provided at his seminar. I was determined to deal with this my way. I kept at it diligently until the following February when it was time to go back for my CT scan. My doctor's appointment for the results was set for April 2007, and this time Bruce was determined to come with me for my appointment.

I started worrying once the CT scan was done. I knew that

whatever would be would be, but it didn't stop the negative thoughts from creeping in. Brain surgery was on my mind 24/7, and I began to obsess about losing a part of myself. I couldn't sleep and found it almost impossible to focus on any one task for any length of time. I just wanted to know one way or another.

Shortly before my scheduled appointment, the doctor's office called to reschedule for May. Talk about frustrating! I tried not to think about it, but I might as well have tried to move a mountain. Those **damn** thoughts would not leave! And then, the evening before my May appointment, the doctor's office called to postpone it again until June. When I got off the phone, I was so furious that I couldn't see or think straight. Common sense was telling me that it wasn't all about me, but I wasn't listening. I called back the next day and talked to the receptionist. I explained that I had been doing the Reiki and visualizations and asked if it was possible to have the doctor look at this year's results and, if there was no change, then I could just wait and come back next year. She called back and told me that she had checked with him and he wanted me to come in. I kept it together on the phone and then explained to her that Bruce was coming in to see the same doctor on another matter in July. Because of the distance and everything else, I asked if it was possible for the two of us to come in at the same time. She agreed, and we set up the appointment more than four months behind having the CT scan done.

Although her comments were non-committal, I worried nonetheless. Perhaps it was just a regular follow-up and protocol dictated that I keep the appointment. Or perhaps it was bad news and surgery was required. My mental roller coaster ride continued until we went in to see him. Bruce's appointment was first. When he was finished with Bruce, he pulled up my results, saw no change, did a few quick reflex tests, and told me to come back next year.

I left his office with a feeling of both elation and anti-climax. I had worked so hard over the past year and had been so tied up in knots about the outcome and then nothing—no change! In a way, it was a huge letdown. I was ecstatic that I had gotten my life back and angry that I had to go through all the mental anguish of not knowing for almost four months, awaiting the results. Over the next few weeks, I debated whether I was ever going back. Bruce, in his maddening realistic way, pointed out that if I did require surgery down the road, I would be better off having a doctor who is one of the best in his field and knew my situation, rather than taking a chance on whoever might be available when I needed them. Sometimes his logic drives me crazy, and I hate it when he's right.

About a month and a half after getting the results from the doctor, we went on a trip to Bowling Green, Kentucky, to meet up with a group from the Corvette Club that we belonged to. It was a great trip, and the day after we got back I started having some dizzy spells and was off balance. I didn't say anything to Bruce the first day, but by the second day, they seemed to be getting worse. It was obvious that something wasn't quite right. I justified it by telling myself and Bruce that I might have an ear infection, but by the third morning it was really bad. I couldn't walk across the room without help. Bruce said he was taking me to the hospital, but I talked him into the local walk-in clinic instead. I figured that if it was the tumor, then I wanted to go St. Michael's Hospital, not Oshawa. When we got to the clinic, it was not open for another hour, so we had no choice but to go to the emergency department at the hospital. We went in and explained the situation. Within five minutes they told us to come back through the doors to the examining room. I went into panic mode when they told us to come in. I started crying, holding on to Bruce, and begging him not to make me go in. I pictured myself coming back out a vegetable. I was sure that they would operate on and lose a part of my brain that would take away my intelligence, memories, and physical abilities! Of course, Bruce insisted that I go in.

The doctor who saw me was excellent and, after some testing, determined that I had an inner ear infection, possibly a virus that I had picked up from the air conditioning while we were away. He advised me on how to deal with it and told me that it would go away within three weeks. Talk about relieved! Bruce teased me about being a big baby at the hospital for almost as long as that darn infection lasted.

All I can say is that the lessons I had already learned from this life were reinforced and solidified: things can change instantly. It could very well have been the tumor, and I would have had to deal with it one way or another. You cannot go back even one minute in time, no matter how hard you wish for it. It gives you more incentive to live in the moment, doesn't it?

The rest of 2007 passed fairly uneventfully, thank goodness, and then early in 2008, Carl, Lois's husband, became ill. A few months later we were burying another brother-in-law. Now two of the five sisters are widows.

The next generation is now getting the wakeup call on the importance of family. Last Thanksgiving, almost every one of the nieces and nephews were here for dinner, and I think it's because they are beginning to realize that we, the moms, dads, aunts and uncles won't always be here. It has become tradition over the past eighteen years for everyone to come to our house for Thanksgiving dinner, and it's been hit and miss as to who shows up. With the five sisters and families, we number more than forty, and as we age the numbers are slowly beginning to dwindle. Over the past few years, I often look around the room and wonder who will not be able to be here next year.

One interesting surprise came out of this past Thanksgiving. Betty informed us that she was going on a cruise with some people she works with in February of 2009. She was trying to talk Mona and me into coming with her, and we told her we would go as long as Lois and Helen would go too. Keep in mind that Lois and Helen have never really traveled and have never been on an airplane before. When we talked about it in the kitchen after supper, it wasn't even a subject that Helen or Lois would discuss, so we dropped it. Later, Mona and I conferred, and we agreed that, with help from Helen's and Lois's families, we could convince them. We got Betty on board, told her to book all five of the sisters for the cruise, and we would present it to Helen and Lois for Christmas. Everything went smoothly until late November when the travel agent sent out a list of all the people who would be going on the cruise. The cat was out of the bag, and, surprisingly, it was Lois who took the most convincing. We had to guilt her into going, and the nice thing was that it was before Karl became ill and he thought it was a good idea and that she should definitely go. Helen put up the tiniest of arguments and quickly agreed. The next thing you know, the Journey of the Five Sisters was set. As I write this, our cruise is seven months away, and all five of us are as excited as can be about it. To have this once-in-a-lifetime opportunity to do something this special while we are all in good health is something that we will all cherish and remember for the rest of our lives!

The winter of 2007–2008 was one of the snowiest years we ever had. Being in the snow-clearing business and not being as young as we used to be made it an extremely difficult winter. Bruce likes to say that he returned from his annual holiday one day in November, got in his truck to plow snow the following day, and the next thing he knew it was spring! The good news was that we made it through and came out the other side. We both put in more hours of work than we have for a long time and keep joking that, at this point in our lives, we're supposed to work smarter, not harder. Nevertheless, here we are in our late fifties and no retirement in sight. I can't imagine myself retired, at least not in the foreseeable future. There are some days when it would be nice to have the house all to ourselves and not worry about clients, employees, or staff being there in our space, but for the most part, we have come to the conclusion that life is pretty good, and, no matter what happens, those left behind do survive and move on. It's the emotional toll on the living who are left behind that is so painful.

I gave in, mostly for Bruce's sake, and went back for my CT scan this year. When the doctor's visit for the results finally came around, he informed me that the tumor is slowly growing, but there is no cause for concern at this point. When I questioned him about waiting for two years for the next CT scan, telling him that I was aware of the symptoms and if I experienced any, I would immediately contact him, he finally consented. I walked out of there with a feeling of relief, vowing not to even think about the damn thing for two years.

Within a couple of weeks, the specialist had fired off a letter to our family doctor, and, the next thing you know, my family doctor was insisting on a checkup. Feeling as if I had no choice, I agreed. Before I left his office, he had convinced me to have a whole host of tests. Right now I am in the midst of having these tests done, and I get really resentful when I think about it. I still have this somewhat-warped and avid distrust of doctors. My rational thinking tells me that it is a deeply instilled perception in my subconscious from earlier experiences, but it persists all the same.

I'm just hoping that my tests come out fine and I can come back to Bruce with an "I told you so," because once again he's trying to change my thinking by pointing out how lucky we are to have such a wonderful family doctor who cares when so many other people are unable to even find a doctor. I know that he's right, but I'm having a hard time telling him so. In the meantime, we will carry on our daily lives and be thankful for each day that we have our health, family, friends, employment, and our sense of humor.

Just this past July, Betty turned sixty years old. As we drove to Belleville for a celebration dinner with her, I kept thinking that I couldn't believe so much time has passed. It seems ludicrous that it's been over fifty years that I've actually known her. The evening was filled with happiness and great memories, and, when we left to come home, it was with a contented sense of family. The only negative thought that I had at all was that I'm next in line to become sixty, but somehow it really doesn't seem all that bad. Just as quickly as Betty turned sixty, she decided to give us a scare by being hospitalized just two days later with gallbladder problems and pancreatitis. Thankfully, she is now on the mend and has just been released from the hospital. Some days it seems like it never ends.

I didn't get a chance to talk to Betty while she was at the hospital, but we have this wonderful relay system in our family: news travels faster than you can imagine! Betty's husband, Ken, used to say, "Telephone, telegraph, tellaMasterson—it's all the same thing." Anyway, after Betty came home from the hospital, I called her to see how she was doing. We had a great conversation, and she has already told me to include this in my story. She shared with me that she now knows what happens when you die! She told me that while she was sick in the hospital she saw Daddy and Ken and that both of them had been children and that Daddy had been wearing little black boots. She also said that I had been there in Heaven, and there were a lot of angels around me weeping. When asked about this interesting bit of information, she told me that the angels were weeping because of the state of the world (I can't say as I blame them) and that I was with the angels and that my purpose is to look after the family. I understood this to be the five sisters, but I still need to clarify that with her.

Now if what Betty claims is true, isn't it interesting that she shared this information on the same day that I finished my book? I don't know if you will find this as freaky as I did, but just go back and reread the first line in chapter 1 that I wrote more than three years ago!

Finishing: August 1, 2005, 3:15 PM

When I started this journey to put everything down on paper, I had no idea that it was going to take me more than three years and three months to complete. Through those numerous incidents that I classify as the tough times in my life, I have almost always written about my feelings to stop myself from going over the deep end. Up until twenty years ago, there were no computers; therefore, I had a basketful of loose notes, as well as many half-started diaries and journals. Compiling these has been an enormous task, but finally I think I've done it. As I suspected, writing this book was very painful, while at other times I would lose track of what I was writing by getting lost in the good memories. Many of the funny moments would have me sitting all by myself and laughing out loud at the pictures going through my head.

As I wrote about many of the family tales, I kept thinking of the stories that Daddy used to tell us when we were young. He loved to tell us over and over again about the chronicles of his life, how Grandma Masterson would sneak him out the back door and through the orchard to school because Grandpa didn't believe in education for farm boys, or how Ma had enticed him one day when he was cutting down trees in the woods by bringing him lunch, and how it was her fault that a few months later there was a shotgun wedding. Coming from a family of six sisters and five brothers gave him an abundance of stories to tell, but we often laughed and made fun of him. I'm sure that I wasn't the only one thinking, "Those were the olden days. Why would we be interested in things that happened before we were even born?"

Today, more than fifty years later, my sisters and brothers and I have achieved that same elderly status. There are our children, now adults, and many of them have children who in the next few years will once again begin another generation. The five sisters in my family are especially close, and we get together often. Thanksgiving is a pretty big deal around here, where everyone tries their best to attend, and is usually held at my house. The five of us with families now number almost forty, which makes it impossible for a formal sit-down dinner. If you were to drop by at Thanksgiving, you would find the driveway and laneway to the shop filled with vehicles. As you made your way up to the house, you would first encounter the smokers out front, visiting and puffing away. As you come through the front door, there would be nothing but a sea of shoes, literally covering every square inch of the front hall floor. Once you waded through the shoe section, peeking left into the office you would find four to six children under the age of ten busy playing office with papers, colored pencils, scissors, and staplers, writing notes to each other about God knows what. Some would be on the phone pretending to deal with customers, while others might be making signs for a neck massage for twenty-five cents or an upcoming play that they were going to perform after supper.

If you looked to your right into the living room, you would see a group of various ages sitting around on whatever surface was available, and more than likely holding a glass of wine or some other drink. The fireplace would be burning, there would be lots of conversation going on, and it would be the most relaxing place to be. Moving through the living room to the sunroom at the back, and you would come across quite a different scenario. Once again you would find everyone perched wherever there was a spot available, and either it would be fairly quiet because they would be in the middle of watching a good movie or else it would be incredibly noisy because someone was playing video games. Glancing out the windows at this point, more than likely there would be some of the younger kids throwing a ball for the dogs or swinging from one of the branches in the tree. If you brought your attention back inside, the next room you would encounter would be the kitchen, which at first glance would appear to be crowded and chaotic. The kitchen table would already have some goodies to munch on until supper was ready. There might be numerous conversations going on, peppered with laughter and teasing. Eventually, the food would get put on every available surface, we'd fill our plates, and find a place to park while we ate. Once we'd eaten so much that we could hardly move, we would sit around moaning and groaning about how full we were and how good the food was.

We're a close-knit family, and, at times like this or any other time that we gather together, at some point one of us will start a sentence with: "Remember the day the big house burned down?" or "That reminds me of the time when Dorothy was five and wanted to be a hairdresser so she cut Susan's hair." Our own stories are as endless as Daddy's were then, and we love to tell them. During these times of reminiscing, I often remember those long-ago feelings of listening to Daddy's stories, and I glance around, keenly aware of the younger generation's eyes beginning to glaze over, and I know exactly what they're thinking. I have at last realized what we put poor Daddy through, and I finally get it. The justification in all this is knowing that in another fifteen or twenty years, this next generation will go through all those same growing pains and conclusions as they attempt to pass on their stories to their children.

Questions I Think I've Been Able to Answer

Is there a possibility of everlasting happiness?

Not everlasting, but definitely intermittently in this lifetime, but one should always have hope!

Where to now?

I will continue to deal with life's problems the way I always have, not looking for trouble, just waiting for it to find me, and then dealing with in the only way that I know how at the time.

In retrospect, do I really think that I can "do it myself"?

Even though the independent part of me would like to think so, my rational mind tells me that I have had guidance from others, both in this physical world as well as from somewhere beyond all the way along. Maybe that's why I've been collecting angels all of these years.

How do I feel now?

As I begin this journey, passing from early middle age to mature middle age, I become keenly aware that my purpose in this life may be only in the infancy stage. I feel that everything up to this point has been preparing me for what is to come.

Why did I write this book?

I truly believe that absolutely everyone has a story to tell. Some of us keep it inside of our heads forever. For me, there was a need to write it down. Maybe it's because in many ways I am detail-oriented. I get angry and frustrated when I don't understand what I'm feeling emotionally. Maybe this book is my way of showing others that you don't necessarily have to voice your feelings—sometimes you can deal with them through other avenues. For me it's by writing about them.

What lessons do I feel I've learned from my sisters?

As you can tell by my story, my five sisters have probably been the biggest influence in my life.

- Lois has taught me patience and how to communicate by asking rather than demanding. I still practice this every day and find it works very well. She also taught me how to make pies and bake.

- Helen has provided me with the gift of humor and acceptance. Although at times she can be embarrassing because you never know what's she's going to say, she is funny and caring and most times even surprises herself with the words that come out of her mouth. I think she has her own devilish "Louie" inside her head.

- Betty has taught me humility. From her I have learned that I don't always get my own way and not to become too big for my britches.

- Mona has taught me forgiveness. Through all of the bullying and mean stunts that I pulled on her when we were younger, she is still one of my best friends, and, as far as I know, she has forgiven me those sins.

A Poem I Wrote for Bruce for Our Twenty-fifth Anniversary, November 21, 1995

The year was nineteen hundred and sixty eight
I moved to Oshawa and sealed my fate
I was fifteen years old and knew it all
Education was to be my primary goal
I got a part time job at the A&W
Where I met a cheeky young man—take a wild guess who
He was known to all only as "Moose"
Hardly anyone knew his real name was Bruce
His reputation was well known all around town
And many who tangled with him ended up on the ground
We fell in love and couldn't wait to be wed
So the marriage certificate took precedence over a new Chev
The wedding was simple—just a few friends and family
In a country church followed by a brief party
Then off on our honeymoon—destination unknown
But finances dictated just one night in Kingston
Then back home to married life and paying the bills
And an unexpected pregnancy when I forgot my pills
That first year was filled with changes and joy
A job at GM for Bruce and a new baby boy
The next two years brought more of a whirl
Buying our first house and a new baby girl
A superintendent in our condominium Bruce did become
He cut the grass, shoveled snow, and kept vandals on the run
A year or so later and enjoying what he was doing now
Bruce branched out and bought an old truck with a plow
Unbeknownst to him, he launched a new career
And no longer had time for fighting and beer
The years rolled on and times were grand
We said good-bye to GM and became a self-employed man
Our lives were filled with camping, mini bikes, and lots of family hours
Normal growing family problems including sunshine, laughter, tears,
and showers

One night in November 1978
At a lottery draw everything went great
Our number was drawn and in that choice
We were the proud owners of half a Rolls Royce
We had our fifteen minutes of fame
Then it was back to work and on with the game
Live was normal and uneventful for the next twelve years
Then tragedy struck and it was a time of tears
Our son was taken from us one December night
Leaving a sorrow so deep, we thought we would never again see the light
That was five short years ago and these past five years have been full of strife
Suddenly our best friend Brian was gone from our life
Leaving another huge hole in both of our hearts
And wondering if our whole world was falling apart
There was a dark time for quite a while and things were a little better it
seemed
Then last January we said good-bye to Bruce's mom known to all as
Grandma Jean
But through the darkness, there is always a light
Fate has a way of intervening and making everything right
Our daughter Andrea is all grown up now and away at school
Education is her priority and partying is her second golden rule
But she still calls us almost every day
Just to say hi and make sure we're okay
She loves to tease Bruce and sometimes drives him wild
Because, you see, he thinks she should settle down and give him a
grandchild
And Bruce found a new love when he turned forty
She's red and flashy and very sporty
But that's okay, I really don't mind
I just wish it did dishes and things of that kind
And only three short weeks ago
Our brother-in-law Tom got lucky at bingo
A fifty thousand dollar check he held in his hand
And it couldn't have happened to a better man
So you see this story has spanned more than twenty-five years
And the changes in our lives are abundantly clear

Dorothy Louise Gagnon

Wonderful families on both sides
Have been our mainstay against changing tides
In family and friends we've been wonderfully blessed
They come from all walks of life and keep us from getting depressed
Of broken dreams and disappointments there have been a few
But another twenty-five years with Bruce is a contract I'll gladly renew

Printed in the United States
148908LV00006B/62/P